HUNTERS ON THE WING
HAWKS

NorthWord

WILDLIFE SERIES

DEDICATION

To watchers everywhere, but especially to "Dirk Vogel," my dad, who marveled at the magic of birds long before it became a pastime for millions.

ACKNOWLEDGMENTS

All of the anecdotes in these chapters are based on first-hand observations in the field, but many details of bird physiology and habits were gleaned from handbooks and research papers by others, particularly those listed in the reference section. Most of these titles were made available to me through the generous cooperation of Dr. Wayne Nelson, raptor enthusiast, falconer, and wildlife biologist with the Alberta Provincial Government.

For encouragement and guidance in writing this book, I am grateful to Barbara Harold, Managing Editor at NorthWord Press, who reviewed the manuscript and made many helpful comments.

Swainson's Hawks migrate farther than other birds, usually flying to Argentina for the winter. Round-trip, their flight totals more than 17,000 miles.

Photography © 1996: Dembinsky Photo Associates: Bill Lea, Cover; Dominique Braud, 16; Mark Thomas, 20-21; Jim Battles, 26; Adam Jones, 33; Anthony Mercieca, 56; Sharon Cummings, 68; Darrell Gulin, 86. National Geographic Society: Bates Littlehales, 2-3; James Amos, 8. Layne Kennedy, 7, 9 (sky), 12-13, 37, 140-141. David Ponton, 9 (hawk). John and Karen Hollingsworth, 11, 48. John Hendrickson, 14, 43, 60, 66, 80, 104, 107, 120, 131. F-Stock: Steve Bly, 18; Henry Holdsworth, 50, 55; Michael Mauro, 88; William Mullins, 114-115. Tom and Pat Leeson, 23, 52-53, 79, 93, 100-101, 117. Paul Rezendes, 29. John Shaw, 30-31, 76-77, 112, 134, 136. C. Allan Morgan, 38, 70, 102, 129. DRK Photo: Marty Cordano, 40-41, 118; John Cancalosi, 90-91, 126; Len Rue Jr., 44; Scott Nielsen, 63; Lewis Kemper, 64-65. The Wildlife Collection: Tom Vezo, 59, 85; Robert Lankinen, 108-109. Michael Quinton, 72, 99, 125. Art Wolfe, 75, 138. Joe McDonald, 82-83. Gerlach Nature Photography, 96, Back Cover. Donna Aitkenhead, 110. Richard Hamilton Smith, 122-123. Rick Poley, 128. Photo/Nats: Sam Fried, 130, 132. Tom Ulrich, 133.

NorthWord Press, Inc.
P.O. Box 1360
Minocqua, WI 54548

Cover design by Ken Hey
Book design by Lisa Moore

Library of Congress Cataloging-in-Publication Data
Dekker, Dick.
    Hawks: hunters on the wing / by Dick Dekker.
          p.   cm.
    Includes bibliographical references (p.   )
    ISBN 1-55971-538-3 (sc)
    1. Hawks —North America. 2. Hawks—North America—Identification. I. Title.
QL696.F32D45   1996
598.9' 16—dc20   95-38566

For a free catalog describing our audio products, nature books and calendars, call **1-800-356-4465**, or write Consumer Inquiries, NorthWord Press, Inc., P.O. Box 1360, Minocqua, Wisconsin 54548

Printed in Hong Kong

HUNTERS ON THE WING
HAWKS

By Dick Dekker

NORTHWORD®

NORTHWORD PRESS, INC.
Minocqua, Wisconsin

Contents

The Red-tailed Hawk is the most common and widespread Buteo. Its extraordinary eyesight enables it to be a fierce and successful predator, even from great distances.

W A T C H E R A T T H E K I L L

overing on the stiff sea breeze, the Kestrel's attention was fixed on something in the grass, thirty feet below. There was an intensity about the little hawk as if its quest were a matter of life or death. Its sharp head resembled the tip of an arrow on the taut bow of quivering wings.

Not far away, one leg slung over a bike saddle, stood a young boy watching the drama unfold in awe, his heart pounding with anticipation.

Suddenly, the Kestrel dropped, feet first, wings arched back. It pounced onto the ground with a vicious thud, flapping for balance. Seconds later, it rose heavily, carrying a small dark item to a fence post. It began to feed at once, holding the prey down with its yellow feet and biting off tiny morsels. Gulping hugely, it swallowed the remainder. Sated, the bird looked at the boy for the first time, bobbed its head and flew away.

Intrigued, as if he had been let in on one of nature's greatest secrets, the kid eagerly went to investigate the wooden post. The weather-worn top showed a small red stain; a bit of gray fur was stuck to the edge. At the base lay a shiny segment of gut, discarded by the Kestrel. Examining it in wonderment, the boy recognized it as an intestine, wet and green like grass.

That was the first time I saw a bird of prey capture a mouse or vole. I can vividly remember what I felt then, half a century ago, for I experience the same obsessive thrill of suspense every time I watch a hawk search for food. The relationship between predators and prey, between the hunters and the hunted, has fascinated me ever since my boyhood days. To me, the few birds of prey that lived around my home represented all that was truly wild and natural. On weekends and holidays I explored low-lying fields and wooded dunes within biking distance from my hometown. Autumn brought great excitement with the arrival of migrating birds from the North.

If flocks of thrushes descended in buckthorn thickets to gorge on overripe berries, I hid nearby to wait for the Sparrowhawk that shadowed its prey. Alerted by the rattling alarm calls of the sentinel birds and the explosive rush of fleeing flocks, I tried to spot the hawk approaching between the bushes. It often showed much cunning and strategy in its attack, but I soon discovered that it could not take a thrush at will. Very few of its hunts terminated in the sudden shriek of a victim.

The predators and the prey are evenly matched in speed and agility, locked in a lethal game of narrow escapes and abrupt endings. Over the eons, while the hunters develop aggressive skills to overtake the prey, the hunted strengthen their defenses to stay ahead of their attackers. Day after day, the lives of wild creatures are dominated by the need to eat and avoid being eaten. The Darwinian concept of the survival of the fittest points two ways: the swifter the hawk, the better its chances of obtaining food; the swifter the thrush, the smaller its chance of becoming that food.

The killing of prey is executed efficiently and speedily by most predators, but there is no denying that it can at times be a protracted and repulsive business. A thrush or sparrow caught by a Cooper's Hawk will die a quick death, but a pheasant expires slowly, and the hawk may begin to pluck its paralyzed victim while it is still alive.

However, the act of killing for food is by no means confined to the predators. The line that separates hunters from the hunted exists only on paper, drawn by scientists who label living things on the basis of physical and evolutionary criteria. The robin that pulls worms out of our lawns, the swallow that chases airborne insects, and the shorebird that stabs aquatic crustaceans are all hunters and killers in their own right. The list of birds and mammals that sustain themselves by exploiting other animal forms is a long one. Each one uses its prey only as food. Like their beauty, their cruelty is in the eye of the beholder.

Those who confess to an affinity for birds of prey run the risk of being accused of a sadistic streak. Ironically, the "hawk lover" may be looked at askance by hunters, who appear unaware of their own paradox that they kill

In typical plumage, Rough-legged Hawks can be easily recognized, but the dark variant can be hard to separate from black Red-tails in the field.

what they love. Most children, who feel the stirring of atavistic hunting instincts, are fascinated by home-made bows and arrows. An old pellet gun may be the greatest of treasures. Mimicking ancient tribal rituals, kids who live close to nature revel in the close company of buddies seeking adventure in the make-believe hunt for small game.

The vast majority of children soon stop hunting and sublimate their primeval needs into bloodless pursuit—chasing a ball, or other competitive sports. Yet, in modern times, city and country people alike are returning to nature for the passive but passionate observation of birds and mammals. Hawks are especially popular. Within a dual framework of admiration and resentment,

Harriers are not above subsisting on carrion, and indeed relish the carcasses of ducks that have died or been shot.

Preceding page: A volunteer releases a newly-banded Kestrel into a migrating flock at Hawk Ridge, Duluth, Minnesota.

perhaps tinged with fear, we have always been fascinated by predators. They give us a chance to escape from the routines of our daily existence, to identify with the hunters, and to take part, albeit vicariously, in their exciting lives, wild and free.

Far from gloating over the anguish of its victim, we as watchers are captivated by the hawk's behavior, its search for prey and the mode of hunting. Of parallel fascination are the reactions of prey species; how they try to avoid being captured, whether they flee or freeze. How a Cooper's Hawk catches a thrush is as interesting as how a thrush manages to cope with a sneaky enemy that may attack at any moment and can do so many times each day.

In recent times, birds of prey have become popular subjects for books, magazines, films and videos, particularly the celebrated falcons and eagles. However, hawks have received far less attention. Why this should be so is a matter of conjecture. They are certainly well-researched by the experts, but seem largely ignored by nature writers and publishers. Therefore, this book is especially dedicated to hawks, the unsung hunters of field and forest.

The number of species portrayed in these chapters include ten common kinds that occur widely on most of the continent: the Marsh Hawk or Northern Harrier, three woodland Accipiters, and six Buteos. Also described are seven not-so-common Buteos whose range is restricted to the south.

Part of the fun and adventure in watching hawks is to learn how to identify the various kinds in the field. All too often we only get an impression, a fleeting glimpse of an elusive flying object, streaking through the forest or disappearing into the distance, too swift or too far away to see much detail. Moreover, there is a confusing variety in adult and immature plumage, and in subspecific and geographic races, particularly in the Buteos.

As pictorial portraits, the fine photographs on these pages speak for themselves, more than a thousand words of description. In addition, the text offers practical hints on field marks. Yet, this publication is not primarily intended as just another identification guide. More complete details on plumage and the differences between species can be found in a number of excellent publications on the market today.

This book focuses on hawk behavior—what they do in their everyday lives, what we can discover by watching them in a natural setting, how they hunt and play, interact and compete. And, above all, how we as watchers react to them.

With a wing-span of four feet and a weight of almost three pounds, the Red-tail is second only to the Ferruginous in size.

HAWKS AND HUMANS

Soaring serenely, the Red-tailed Hawk spirals upward to join its mate that circles in the opposite direction. They seem to stitch the clouds together with ephemeral artistry. Their rakish silhouettes become smaller and smaller, dark specks against white, a faint blur on the blue, spring sky. Their high-pitched calls drift down to the watcher below.

Lying on our backs in the grass, sheltered from the fresh breeze and resting from a long walk, we are mesmerized by the intertwining aerial ballet overhead, high among the clouds. Hawks seem so far above aching feet and worldly worries. In our noisy aircraft, we may fly faster and higher than any hawk. Yet, traveling on foot over rough ground, struggling through mud or tangled thickets, we gaze with a sense of wonder, envy perhaps, at the effortless soaring of birds.

MESSENGERS OF THE GODS

From the dawn of our consciousness, primitive peoples, who did not know the power of a propeller, must have looked upon hawks and eagles as favorites of the gods.

Evidence of hawk worship and totemism can be found among aboriginals on all continents. In Australia, Malaysia, India, Mongolia, Japan and Africa, birds of prey were venerated as deities and messengers from the spirit world whose help was implored in raising crops, hunting wild game or in warfare. In

Red-tails catch a surprising number of moles and pocket gophers by patiently waiting near the mounds of excavated soil that mark their underground retreats.

the tropical forests of Borneo, wooden images of hawks stood in front of tribal houses to ward off evil powers. On the twisting byways of South America, modern-day truck drivers still hang the dried feet of an eagle or hawk over the windshield as a charm to stave off accidents. Peruvian natives used to smear their bodies with the juice of boiled hawk talons before setting out to hunt in the mountains. Indians of the Amazon and Ecuador fitted their arrows with hawk feathers so that they would go as swiftly and surely to their mark as a winged predator.

Birds of prey received exalted attention in the civilizations of ancient Egypt, Babylonia and Assyria, as is plain from opulent decorations on temples and tombs. The ancient kingdoms of Egypt knew many taloned gods, their stone images guarding ruins unearthed from desert sands. In Israel and Palestine, the sermons of the prophets were spiced with imagery of predatory birds, of eagles soaring over the House of the Lord, of hawks finding their way in the heavens by divine direction, or of vultures gathering over battle.

In the Americas, the condor was held in high esteem by Incas, Mayas and

Aztecs, which is plain from numerous artistic images on their pottery and jewelry. Condor feathers, tied to a stick, were considered a source of supernatural powers, used in rituals to heal the sick. Among aboriginal peoples from the Andes to the Rocky Mountains, feathers of eagles decorated the headgear of warriors and chiefs as status symbols or ceremonial totems.

Next to sun worship, nearly all prairie Indians believed in the Thunderbird, which signified many things to different tribes. Haunting the realm of clouds over the skyline, the great eagle unleashed thunderstorms by flapping its wings together; its flashing eyes produced the lightning. Coastal tribes in western Canada believed that the Thunderbird had created the world and that it caught whales in its claws, devouring them on mountain tops.

Curiously similar legends of great mythical eagles derive from Tibet, India and Burma, as well as from Brazil and the Cook Islands. In ancient Greece, Zeus, the paramount religious deity, ruled the sky. He commanded thunder and lightning and dwelled with eagles on Mount Olympus.

Quite apart from its spiritual significance, the Golden Eagle has been a symbol of earthly power since the age of Belshazzar of Babylon, in the sixth century B.C. In more recent times, it became the heraldic emblem of Roman Caesars, Russian Tsars and Austrian Emperors. It is indeed fitting and a matter of pride, that the splendid Bald Eagle, which only occurs in North America and has a continent-wide distribution, should have become the emblem of the United States.

A HAWK ON THE FIST

Over the millennia, while birds of prey have played a deeply significant but largely symbolic role in the spiritual lives of people across the world, there was a time when their practical use was more important; this was the age of falconry. It involved the training of predatory birds as winged allies of human hunters in the pursuit of game. Primarily as a means of capturing wild meat for the table, the practice originated in Asia, perhaps as far back as four thousand years ago. During the Middle Ages, the art of taming hawks was brought to Europe by the Crusaders and became "The Sport of Kings," a fashionable pastime at royal courts and country estates that lasted for centuries.

From Austria to Britain, the care and training of hawks pervaded everyday life for a wide array of citizens, who took their prized pets along to all social functions, including church. References to hawks and hawking featured prominently in the literature of the time. Shakespeare frequently used birding terms and analogies that are still in use today. Words such as "coward," "haggard" and "quarry" were derived from falconry. So are the expressions "in a towering rage," "beating around the bush," "taken by surprise" and "as vulnerable as a sitting duck." The meaning of these words and phrases may have widened, but were originally restricted to the interaction of raptorial birds and their prey.

The invention of the shotgun eventually spoiled much of the profit and fun of flying hawks, but the practice enjoys a strong resurgence today, with thousands of devotees in the United States and Canada, as well as in Europe and Asia. How does falconry actually work? How do humans manage to control and cooperate with these wild and fiercely independent creatures?

At its best, the sport is still conducted the way it was centuries ago, using a minimum of artificial tools or equipment. In a sense, the captive hawk or falcon is controlled by its stomach. Taken from the wild when young, or obtained from experts who nowadays breed hawks in captivity, the bird is habituated to people, until it is docile enough to sit on a gloved hand and receive food from its trainer. Eventually, it is allowed to fly free, but only if it is hungry, so that it can be expected to return quickly if offered a piece of meat.

Traditionally, the food is tied onto a "lure," a facsimile of a bird attached to a line that can be swung around or thrown up into the air, allowing the hawk to see it from afar. The lure is weighted down with wood or metal, preventing the hawk from carrying it away, after it has "captured" the lure.

When it is fully trained, a falcon is let go only after game has been spotted by the falconer, often with the assistance of a pointer dog. The intended quarry can be a covey of partridges, hiding in the grass, or ducks on a pond. As long as the falcon is above them in the air, winging back and forth, climbing ever higher, the partridges do not dare to fly, and the ducks stay put on the water where they are safe from the falcon. To give the falcon a sporting chance in the air, the human partners have to come into action.

Shouting and gesticulating, the falconer runs up to scare the partridges or ducks from their hiding place. Often the job is done by a dog, a spaniel or other hunting breed, that has been waiting eagerly for the order. The moment of

Preceding page: Perhaps the prettiest of our Buteos, some adult Red-shoulders are as red as a robin. All have bright yellow feet.

truth arrives as soon as the target is airborne and the falcon makes its move, descending at a steep angle. A good falcon quickly overtakes the fleeing prey, but the intended victim may dodge or reach cover just in time. To create the best opportunity for success, the falconer and his helpers attempt to flush the quarry over open country at the right moment, when the hawk is coming into a favorable position for attack, maximizing its chances. Doing what it does by instinct, the falcon strikes the prey down or seizes it with its feet.

Other kinds of predatory birds such as the Goshawk are let go in a more direct method, as soon as a pheasant or rabbit is sighted in the open, not too far away. Unlike a falcon, the powerful and versatile Goshawk is a short-range sprinter that does not hesitate to seize its prey in the bushes, as well as in the air or even in shallow water. Other species popular for falconry are Cooper's Hawks, Red-tails and Harris' Hawks.

At a maximum weight of just over two pounds, a Goshawk is more than ten times as heavy as a small Sharp-shinned Hawk. Yet, their hunting strategies are very similar, combining active search with stealth and surprise.

The successful hawk or falcon, standing defiantly on its catch, should allow its master to approach closely, enticing it with a tidbit of fresh meat, while the quarry is spirited away into the game bag. If worked with skill, a well-trained hawk can capture a succession of prey. However, it is not always easy to locate suitable targets, and some modern-day falconers are content if their birds manage to capture pigeons released under them. Falcons that fail to catch anything may fly away and become lost.

As an insurance that a hawk can be located, even if it has flown out of sight, modern falconers equip their birds with tiny radio-transmitters attached to their tail or legs. At the end of the day, all falconers are pleased if they succeed in calling the bird back down. Secured by a leather strap attached to its feet, the precious hunter is taken home again, where it sits on its block until the next outing. To keep them in good shape, hawks should be flown every day, a demanding task for busy falconers.

From the start, falconry requires infinite patience and skill, and some money. Many of its followers are quite fanatical, claiming that their sport is an advanced form of bird watching. It is indeed rewarding, and the culmination of many days of effort, to see a well-trained bird capture its prey. The victories are all the more sweet because they come at a certain risk. Birds often escape over the skyline or die prematurely by disease or accident, ending the dream and forcing the falconer to begin the training process all over again with another hawk.

By contrast, the watcher of wild hawks does not have to own the object of his or her affection, and there is no investment of time and money in acquiring or keeping a bird. To see a hawk or falcon, wild and free, on the prowl for prey is one of nature's most exciting shows, and it is available without charge to any patient and lucky observer.

PERSECUTION AND PROTECTION

Bird watching has soared in popularity—a recent estimate of the binocular-carrying crowd in North America stands around 30 million! Hawks are keenly appreciated and their correct identification in the field holds challenge for novice and expert alike. But their legal protection was slow in coming.

In 1955, Roger Tory Peterson, arguably the world's most prominent bird watcher, declared himself pessimistic about the future of hawks. In his foreword to Alexander Sprunt's *North American Birds of Prey*, he comments on the increasing scarcity of many species and particularly the steady decline of the Bald Eagle. "It seems reasonable to assume that if the present trend continues, the United States may before long face the prospect of being represented by an extinct emblem."

"The raptores, of all birds the finest, are like masterworks of art," Peterson wrote. Yet, their legal protection had to wait a very long time. In the past, shooting and trapping of hawks was common practice all over the country. Even in 1918, when most birds were protected by the Migratory Bird Treaty between Canada and the United States, hawks, owls and vultures were omitted.

Alexander Sprunt was equally pessimistic about the future of hawks and deplored their wholesale slaughter at the hands of gunners. But little did he and his fellow ornithologists know about a far worse calamity that was just about to hit the bird watcher's world: the poisonous pesticides.

During the 1950s, residues of persistent organo-chlorine insecticides used in agriculture, particularly DDT, were accumulating in songbirds, waterfowl and fish. The poisons reached to even higher levels in the birds of prey, which are at the top of the food chain, resulting in direct mortality of adults and chicks as well as sterility in eggs. Some species, such as the Peregrine Falcon, Sharp-shinned Hawk, Bald Eagle and Osprey, quite suddenly began disastrous declines that shocked the world.

Finally, in 1972, restrictions were placed on the use of DDT and other highly toxic agents. In the same year, all birds of prey received the protection of federal laws as well as some state legislation. Since then, a major turnaround has been achieved and some of the formerly affected species have been brought back from the brink of disaster. The Bald Eagle again nests within sight of the White House, and Peregrines are flying again in many states, a direct result of an innovative program of breeding them in captivity. Hundreds of barn-raised Peregrines have been turned free, repopulating former haunts and now breeding on their own.

The return of the Peregrine is one of the most heart-warming conservation stories of our time, its success due in great part to the falconers, whose ancient knowledge and methods were utilized to make it happen. The Peregrine story has received much publicity and raised the status of all birds of prey. Appreciation and tolerance for predatory birds have never been greater, boding well for their future.

Red-tails like to sit on prominent perches to advertise their presence to other Red-tails,
and as an energy-efficient method of scouting for prey.

Part I

R E A P I N G   T H E   W I N D

Except for some spectacular species, such as the adult Bald Eagle, birds of prey are difficult to tell apart in the field. Most are closely related and resemble each other in size, shape and plumage, with minor differences that make their correct identification a challenge, even for the expert.

Why are there so many species of hawks? To find out and gain understanding, adding perspective to our hawk watching pleasure, we must go back to the beginning.

THE FEATHERED LIZARD

Birds are among the finest examples of nature's creative genius. Imagine a lowly lizard crawling on the dirt. How could this ground-hugging creature ever soar among the clouds? Yet, evolution's engineers did it. They not only produced the flap-and-sail Pterodactyls of the dinosaur era, but they turned scales into feathers! A marvel of construction, the feather became the building block, combining strength with lightness of weight, for the varied and colorful avian treasury we know today. Like the bones of birds, the shafts of feathers are hollow. The pinions of the largest species are serrated along the outer edges for extra stiffness. The smaller feathers can be completely waterproof with a wonderful insulating quality that protects even the smallest birds from the cold of winter nights.

Although the fossil record is fragmentary, scientists believe that primitive versions of feathered birdlike creatures developed far back in geological time, perhaps 138 million years ago. Hawks as we know them today evolved 30 to 40 million years ago, in the Tertiary Period, from the same flying lizards that became the ancestors of the dinosaurs.

Modern birds still show vestiges of their reptilian ancestry. The embryonic feather, in the early stages of its growth, resembles a scale. Vestigial claws can be detected on the wings of ducks and geese. Birds of prey have a prominent alula (or thumb wing), a movable segment of the carpal joint that comes into play during soaring and hovering. Other reptile-like characteristics of birds include the egg tooth of chicks, which drops off after it has served its function, and the so-called third eye lid that can be closed as a protective membrane.

The largest birds of prey evolved in the Pleistocene. Skeletons extracted from the famous Rancho la Brea tar pits in California show that the Teratorais condor had a wingspan of 14 feet, twice as large as the Bald Eagle. Another species, of which only one wing bone was found, is believed to have been even bigger, up to 20 feet in diameter. Historians speculate that a few of these huge raptors may have survived up to a fairly recent epoch, late enough to have given rise to the Thunderbird legends of Plains Indians.

WHAT'S IN A NAME?

Of more than nine thousand avian species known in the world, 287 are classified as birds of prey. Not counting the night-hunting owls, North America is home to 33 diurnal raptors. An additional six or seven are occasional visitors from other continents. In the scientific nomenclature, all birds of prey belong to the order of Falconiformes. Based on physical characteristics and evolutionary relationships, they have been divided into the following families and subfamilies: Vultures, Ospreys, Kites, Harriers, Accipiters, Buteos, Eagles and Falcons.

But what defines a bird of prey? Is it a bird that eats other living creatures? In fact, so do practically all species. Even the most persistent vegetarians, such as seed-eating finches and sparrows, switch to insect food when there are young in the nest. Dabbling ducks, content to slobber vegetable matter for most of the year, crave a high-protein diet of aquatic insects and crustaceans prior to the demanding task of laying a clutch of oversized eggs.

All members of the hawk family, including the Harris' Hawk, have strongly curved bills. The oval-shaped nostrils are located on a fleshy section of the upper mandible called the cere.

A better definition of a bird of prey is found in its habit of capturing food with its taloned feet that are well-designed for holding down and killing prey. The term "raptor," in general use today, is therefore a more precise designation. It is derived from the Latin *rapere* which means "seize."

Interestingly, the Teutonic roots of the word "hawk" are *haf* or *hab* which means *greifen* (seize) in modern German. Fittingly, a bird of prey is a *Greifvogel* in Germany, and the Goshawk is called *Habicht*. Dutch and Swedish equivalents are *havik* and *hök*.

The ancient Anglo-Saxon root of hawk was *havoc*, a concept that has a much different connotation today, but the havoc caused by a Goshawk that darts out of the trees and drops like a bomb among a farmer's chickens can be easily imagined.

The Goshawk is the largest member of the *Accipiters*, which are agile forest hawks with long tails and relatively short wings. By contrast, the group that goes by the Latin name *Buteo* includes slow-flying, open country birds with broad wings for soaring and stubby tails.

In England, the term "hawk" was and is restricted to the Accipiters—that include two species in western Europe (Goshawk and Sparrowhawk), and three in North America (Northern Goshawk, Cooper's Hawk, and Sharp-shinned Hawk).

Unfortunately, the European farmers who settled in the New World three centuries ago branded all raptorial birds as hawks and attached the Goshawk's rapacious reputation also to beneficial open-country species such as the Buteos. To early American country folk, there were only big "chicken hawks" and little "chicken hawks," and the only good one was a dead one.

Today, the word "hawks" continues to be used for birds of prey collectively. However, in recent years, sanctioned by the American Ornithologists' Union, the falcons have been rechristened. The former Duck Hawk, Pigeon Hawk and Sparrow Hawk, which belong to the long-winged falcon tribe, are now known, respectively, as Peregrine, Merlin and American Kestrel. And the former Marsh Hawk is now called Northern Harrier.

Thus far, the name "hawk" has stuck to the Buteos, although their English name was Buzzard, which, again erroneously, was given to the American vultures. Worldwide, the genus *Buteo* includes at least 24 members, of which about half occur in North America. With broad wings and short tails, the

Preceding page: Red-tailed Hawks can be found both in deciduous forests and open country, including prairies, plains, tundra and farmlands.

Northern Harriers have a varied diet, usually consisting of mice, rats, frogs and small mammals.

Buteos are expert soarers. Some of them prefer woodlands, others wide-open prairies or arctic tundras. Each species is well-adapted to its preferred habitat niche and local range of prey. The Buteo hawks are the most common and visible of the raptors, especially on migration hotspots where crowds of bird watchers gather to marvel at the spectacle of hawks overhead.

MIGRANTS ON THE MOVE

During fall, from early September to well into November, many species of diurnal raptors travel down the continent to winter in warmer climates, some going as far as Central and South America. The migrants move along a broad front. However, if they encounter obstacles such as the Great Lakes, the Atlantic Ocean, or mountain chains, they hesitate to cross and are diverted. Following some of these "guiding lines," depending on wind direction and the formation of updrafts, the travelers become more concentrated as they go.

The most famous hawk highway parallels the Appalachians, the rugged spine of the continent that runs from Quebec to Alabama. Leisurely soaring and sailing their way down the foothills and ridges, the mass movement of raptors has attracted the attention of people for hundreds of years. In the days when the killing of hawks was a common pastime, shooting parties were traditional along the Appalachians, and thousands upon thousands of hawks, eagles and falcons were destroyed each fall. At some spots, the carnage continued until 1956 when protective state laws finally came into effect.

However, at one point along the mountain chain, the National Audubon Society was successful in turning a former raptor slaughter ground into an internationally celebrated migration hotspot: the famous Hawk Mountain Sanctuary along the Kittatinny Ridge in Pennsylvania. Each fall since then, crowds of visitors scan the skies through binoculars or scopes to tally passing hawks, eagles, ospreys, vultures and falcons that can add up to thousands per day.

The hawks are late starters, generally not moving much until rising air currents begin to form and tail winds are blowing, facilitating soaring and sailing. Depending on weather conditions, some days are far better than others. On one exceptional date, September 16, 1948, the lookout was passed by nearly twelve thousand hawks. Taking count each day during the migration season, year after year, and comparing total sightings over the decades, places such as Hawk Mountain have been compiling a fantastic amount of data that is useful as population indices for several species of raptors.

The first hawks to come down from the North are nearly all Broad-wings, soaring high on warm September days. The greatest variety, including Accipiters, Northern Harriers, Bald Eagles, Ospreys and falcons, passes through during October. The majority of Red-tails, Red-shoulders, Goshawks and Golden Eagles migrate during November, with a few stragglers continuing until early December.

During midday, especially on warm days, there often seems to be a lull in the passage of hawks, which has puzzled bird watchers for years. It is now thought that many birds may escape detection simply by flying too high to be seen with the naked eye. High-soaring birds may also be less inclined to follow the so-called "guiding lines" of the landscape far below.

As disclosed by radio-tracking, most Accipiters and Buteos travel at altitudes between one and three thousand feet. But airplane pilots have reported Broad-wings and Swainson's Hawks as high as 11,000-13,000 feet over Panama. Vultures and condors, as well as some hawks, have even been recorded at 15,000-20,000 feet.

The use of tiny radio-transmitters, attached to a bird's legs, tail or back, is beginning to provide a wealth of good information on travel times and distance covered. A Sharp-shinned Hawk captured at Cedar Grove, Wisconsin, on October 9, 1971, flew to Alabama in eleven days—a distance of 750 miles. Red-tailed Hawks tracked in California flew mean daily distances of about 40 miles to a maximum record of 120 miles.

A new window to the riddles of migration was opened by the recent invention and application of satellite telemetry. Equipment packages have now been reduced in weight to less than one ounce, making them light enough to be carried by birds. Eagles fitted with these devices are tracked via satellite to their winter quarters in Africa and back to Latvia and Kasachstan for distances exceeding 4,000 miles. Researchers in Alaska have recently applied this technology to Peregrine Falcons, which were followed from northern nesting grounds to wintering habitats in Texas and beyond.

Other technical research has revealed that some migrating Peregrines continue their migrations at night and do not hesitate to travel over the ocean. These fascinating facts were discovered after several falcons were fitted with tiny conventional transmitters and tracked by vehicle or light aircraft. The falcons left Maryland and Virginia headlands over the open ocean to make the crossing to Cuba, three to four hundred miles out at sea. Pushed by tail winds, the birds remained airborne during the night when warm air currents over the water allowed them to soar and sail.

The capture of migrating hawks is routine at several migration hotspots where people set up traps or nets baited with a sparrow, starling or pigeon. A hungry or playful hawk that makes a pass at the decoy ends up entangling itself. The numbers involved can be very large. For instance, at Duluth, Minnesota, between 1973 and 1978, a total of 11,515 Sharp-shins were caught. They were released after having been classified, measured, weighed and fitted with numbered leg bands. Between 1971 and 1982, bird-banders at Hawk Cliff, Ontario, captured 15,509 Sharp-shins, as well as several thousand Red-tails, Cooper's Hawks and Goshawks. The total number of raptors caught and banded at Cape May Point, New Jersey, between 1967 and 1992 was 81,000. At other spots, Assateague Island in Maryland, and at Padre Island in Texas, hundreds of Peregrine Falcons are banded each fall.

The objective of all this field research on migrating hawks is to obtain answers on some basic questions about population dynamics. Where do the birds come from? Where are they going? And, most importantly, are our birds of prey declining or increasing in number? Over four decades, since the early 1950s, comparative data have varied greatly and need to be interpreted with caution. By and large, some hawks seem to have maintained themselves well or are even increasing. However, woodland species such as Broad-wings and Sharp-shins appear to be on the decline, probably as a direct result of deforestation in their northern nesting habitat and a shrinking prey base.

MIGRATION HOTSPOTS

Moving southward down the Appalachian chain in a thickening stream, migrating raptors concentrate at numerous hawk watching lookouts, with the better sites averaging from 25 to more than 100 birds seen per hour. Some of the most popular hotspots are Mount Tom in Massachusetts, and Raccoon Ridge in New Jersey. On the Pennsylvania side of the Kittatinny Ridge, major hotspots are Little Gap, Bake Oven Knob and Hawk Mountain. There are many good lookouts in West Virginia, such as Rockfish Gap, Bear Rocks, and Rogersville-Hanging Rock Fire Tower. Kyle Ford Fire Tower is a productive site in Tennessee. Farther south, migrants come through in low concentrations with a hotspot at Lookout Mountain in Georgia.

Hawk Ridge in Duluth, Minnesota, is a popular spotting location over the Lake Superior fly-way.

To watchers in the Southwest, it is a thrill to see the uncommon Zone-tailed Hawk.

Other major hawk highways parallel lakes and oceans, where the migrants hesitate to fly over water and are channeled along the shore. On the Atlantic seaboard, sightings increase from Briar Island in Nova Scotia to the New England coast. Good lookouts are Lighthouse Point in New Haven, Connecticut, and particularly Cape May Point in New Jersey, where as many as 25,000 hawks have been recorded on a single day! Thousands of Accipiters and falcons pass by Long Island's barrier beaches. Further south, local hotspots are at Kiptopeke in Virginia and Fort Johnson in South Carolina. Migrations continue along the Florida Keys with several productive observation points.

Some hotspots along the Gulf Coast are Baton Rouge, Louisiana, the Texas Coastal Bend and the Corpus Christi region. Along the Great Lakes, large autumn flights occur at many locations, such as Hawk Cliff in Ontario, Cedar Grove in Wisconsin, and Duluth and Hawk Ridge Nature Reserve in

Minnesota. By contrast, migrations across the Great Plains and the Rocky Mountains seem to take place over a broad front, with some concentrations along the foothills in Alberta and Montana. A good lookout along the Pacific Coast is at the Golden Gate Raptor Observatory in California.

As soon as weather conditions allow, raptors that have survived the hazards of winter begin the long journey back to their breeding territories. Again moving across a broad front, spring migrants seldom reach the same spectacular concentrations of autumn. Noted exceptions are along the southern shores of Lakes Erie and Ontario, and on Lake Superior at Whitefish Point in Michigan. Braddock Bay or Derby Hill in New York State are also autumn hotspot sites. Along the eastern escarpment of the Rocky Mountains, from Montana to Alberta, several thousand Golden Eagles are counted each March and April. Impressive movements of Buteos and Accipiters can be seen at numerous other points across the nation, depending on the vagaries of wind and weather, and many good hotspots may remain to be discovered.

For detailed information on hawk watching locations in your area, contact: The Hawk Migration Association of North America, 3094 Forest Acre Trail, Salem, Virginia 24153; Hawk Watch International, P.O. Box 660, Salt Lake City, Utah 84110-0660; or your local Audubon Society.

To Each its Own

Why are there so many kinds of hawks? The answer is simple: to take advantage of many kinds of prey in many different habitats. But how did these highly territorial and aggressive animals work out their differences? By a slow, inexorable process of segregation—through the twin forces of adaptive modifications and resource partitioning. How and why this is accomplished was first explained in the monumental treatise *Origin Of Species*, published in 1859 by renowned British naturalist Charles Darwin.

As an example of his theories of evolution and natural selection, Darwin described a group of finches that had been geographically isolated on the remote Galapagos Islands for an unknown length of time. All finches look much the same except for the size and shape of their bills; some have stubby beaks, others long, thin or curved mandibles. According to Darwin, after the first finches arrived on

the Galapagos, perhaps blown across the ocean from South America, they began using a variety of local foods. Some gathered plant seeds, others hunted insects, or collected nectar from flowers. The beaks of each group slowly diverged from the ancestral norm and became specialized foraging utensils that were passed on to their offspring. In this way, by better utilization of a wide spectrum of food resources, the total number of finches on the islands was allowed to expand greatly.

Similar physical changes have affected the birds of prey. From a primitive prototype, the many varieties existing today have been molded by food habits and habitat. Each species restricted itself to a different ecological niche, thereby reducing inter-specific competition between them. They even have a night-shift—the owls—that become active after diurnal raptors leave the field.

Some birds of prey, such as the vultures, feed mainly on carrion. The singular Osprey preys on fish. But most of the other species take either birds or mammals. It stands to reason that predators of birds need to be faster than predators of mammals; hence their respective physiques should be quite different.Pursuing birds in flight over open terrain and high in the sky, the falcon tribe evolved long, narrow wings designed for sustained power. However, high speed comes at the expense of maneuverability, and vice-versa. At the last moment, the intended quarry of a falcon often manages to escape by dodging sharply, forcing its pursuer to overshoot the mark. If the falcon is keen, it may start the chase all over again. But if the prey reaches the cover of bushes or trees, the falcon will have to give up; with its long wings it is not built for flying through dense woods.

By contrast, bird predators that live in the forest such as the Accipiters have relatively short wings with rounded tips, excellent for quick acceleration and sudden bursts of speed. Their tails are long, facilitating hairpin turns and instant stops. The trade-off lies in the Accipiter's inability to maintain top speed for longer than a few minutes.

The Buteos, which hunt mainly mammals, have sacrificed somewhat, both in speed and maneuverability, but they gained on wing size, allowing for

Preceding page: The Ferruginous' major prey consists of small mammals, from mice to hares, but this powerful hawk manages to take a wide variety of birds as well, by catching them on the ground.

While hunting over dense ground cover, Harriers detect prey by acoustical clues as well as sight. Their peculiar facial ruff, reminiscent of owls, hides unusually large ear openings.

energy-efficient soaring while on the lookout for prey far and near. Buteos are partial to hunting over terrain where vegetation is short and prey is easily spotted.

Where the grass is tall and in reedy marshes, another specialized mammal hunter comes into its own: the Northern Harrier. Cruising very low over the ground, its large wings held at an uptilted angle and the long tail give it great buoyancy at slow speeds and instant pouncing control when it suddenly comes across prey in the grasstop jungle below.

DIVIDING THE BOOTY

Falcons, Accipiters, Buteos and Harriers have been wonderfully successful in taking their distance from each other, so to speak, through morphological

The Northern Goshawk is a fierce predator. They have been known to steal game from hunters and chickens from farmers, even while the humans were present.

differences in the skeleton, muscles, wings and tail, affecting their powers of flight. Within each genus, direct competition was reduced further by partitioning of prey and habitat niche.

For instance, by and large the three Accipiters have divided the feathered booty of the forest by size. At twice the weight of the Cooper's Hawk, and more than six times heavier than the Sharp-shin, the Goshawk can take larger prey than the other two members of this rapacious clan. During nesting time, additional separation of foraging range is a result of the Goshawk's preference for old forests with big trees, while the Sharp-shin does not mind nesting in shrubby thickets. Also, the Goshawk has a more northerly breeding distribution than the Cooper's Hawk.

Compared to the Accipiters, members of the genus *Buteo* are much closer in weight range, and they subsist mostly on the same kinds of small rodents, rabbits and squirrels. To partition their food sources, the Buteos go by a strategy that biologists call "spatial segregation." While the Red-shouldered Hawk prefers marshy woods, the Swainson's soars over wide open prairies, and the Red-tail frequents park-like landscapes.

Nevertheless, in mixed habitats inter-specific competition for nesting sites and hunting range among Buteos can be fierce, especially if tree cover is altered by human land-use patterns. Despite nature's clever designs at keeping them apart, different species of hawks often interact. Hostile encounters between these heavily armed and aggressive creatures are always interesting to watch, particularly attempts at food piracy. Kleptoparasitism, as it is officially called, is an everyday occurrence, with the more powerful raptors stealing prey from the smaller and slower ones. The big ones may even kill and eat their smaller kin, or rob their young out of the nest, treating them just like any other prey. In the final analysis, all hawks live by the same motto: "might makes right."

THE GREAT PROVIDERS

When you see a pair of raptors together, soaring over their nesting territory, it is usually obvious that one is bigger than the other. Quite unlike most other avian and mammalian species, the smaller one is the male. This curious phenomenon is termed "reversed sexual dimorphism." Simply stated, it means that females are larger than males. In some species, such as the Sharp-shinned Hawk, the difference can be considerable; she can be up to double his weight. In falcons, males are about one third lighter than females of the same geographic race.

Generally, the size difference between the sexes is greatest in bird predators, and least in species that subsist mainly on mammals or insects. It is nonexistent in vultures, where males may be even bigger than females. But why this should be so continues to be a subject of intense scientific debate. Half a dozen different theories have been postulated and scores of papers have been written about this puzzling question.

A prominent hypothesis involves the same principle as in the separation of the species: resource partitioning. Just as members of the same species compete for food, so would the partners of a breeding pair if they were the same size. On the other hand, if the female is bigger, she can take larger prey than her mate, reducing competition between them and effectively widening the pair's prey base in their territory.

It has also been argued that small males are better providers, since they require less food for themselves and are more successful at capturing prey of a size that can be carried to the nest. This notion certainly appears to be correct in the case of open-country bird hunters such as the Peregrine and the Merlin. Based on my field observations of about two thousand hunting flights, the falcons achieved an overall success rate of between 10 and 12 percent. But the adult males did much better than the average. Pursuing small shorebirds and passerines (perching and songbirds), they managed to catch one out of every three or four chased.

In Goshawks, it is known that breeding females, prior to egg-laying, put on 10 or 20 percent more body weight, making them lethargic and less effective as hunters than the much lighter and agile males. An alternative and complementary theory explaining reversed sexual dimorphism is that bigger females are better breeders. Because of their larger body size, they can lay bigger eggs, have more body heat for incubation, and are better at defending the nest against rivals and potential nest robbers.

Both of the above scenarios appear to make sense and may operate at the same time. Through evolution, each sex appears to have reached its optimal size. The male increased his foraging efficiency by becoming as small as he can afford to be, while the female maximized her bulk and her brood's chances for survival in the unconscious knowledge that a larger mother is a better mother.

Usually, both sexes take part in nest building and raising the young, protectively defending them against all potential enemies, be they avian, mammalian or even human. The fury of a mother Goshawk aimed at an intruder is frightening to experience firsthand. Many a novice bird-bander or egg-collector has been slashed on the head, or almost knocked out of the nest tree.

Less dangerous but equally vehement is the defensive behavior of a pair of Red-tailed Hawks, protesting a person's approach from afar. Having learned to keep their distance from people by past persecution, the hawks are too timid to make a direct attack but their anxiety is plain to see and hear as they fly about restlessly, calling constantly.

In the early stages of incubation, the male provides his partner with all her needs. He eagerly takes turns brooding the eggs if she has to leave for a few moments. Later, when the chicks can be left alone, the female does her share of foraging for the growing brood.

Weeks or even months after they have fledged, the youngsters are still attended by both parents. With plenty of time for play, they enjoy a long apprenticeship, learning to be hawks, and reap the wind, the wide world at their command. When they finally soar free into the clouds, supreme examples of nature's creativity, they lift the spirits of all of us who take a moment to look up in wonder at hawks overhead.

Northern Harrier nests are built mainly on the ground in tall weeds or grasses on a platform of sticks, usually near a swamp or marsh.

Part II

HAWKS AT HOME AND ON THE HUNT

Hawks resemble each other in many aspects of their physiology and behavior, such as the shape of their bills, feet and claws. The bare skin of legs and the base of the bill is always yellow—brightest in the adults, palest in immatures. Hawk voices are similar too, shrill and strident, not at all what we might call musical. The most commonly heard call of all Accipiters, when disturbed near the nest, is a staccato cacking. The Buteos utter their displeasure in a hoarse, grating scream.

The family life of all hawks shows similarities as well. In all hawks, the female lays three to six eggs and does most of the brooding, which takes about four weeks. All chicks are hatched in helpless condition, nearly blind and unable to stand or keep their large heads erect for long, but they are not naked. Covered in whitish down, they need the protection of the parent to keep warm, until their own coats thicken. Fed with great care at first, the young have voracious appetites and gain rapidly in size, multiplying their hatching weight more than thirty times in four to six weeks.

It is best to leave hawks alone during the time when they are tending eggs or small chick. Disturbance by people can result in lethal chilling or desertion of the nest. It is far better to observe hawks from a distance, so that their behavior is natural and uninhibited by our presence.

Northern Harrier

Winging its way against the prairie breeze, the Harrier skimmed over the uneven ground, veering and rolling like a sailboat on ocean waves. Head bent sharply down, its eyes were scrutinizing the grassy jungle just below, ears attuned to the slightest rustle or squeak. Suddenly, tail fanning wide, the bird checked itself and plunged down in a lightning-quick somersault. A hit! Or so it seemed. Flapping its wings for balance and hopping up and down, it looked as if its prey was putting up a stiff fight. Two, three other Harriers approached hurriedly and landed nearby, intent on sharing the kill.

Watching the little drama through binoculars, curious to find out what kind of bird or mammal the Harrier had caught, I slowly walked closer. The "killer" was the last to flush. In its long clutches it carried a small object but dropped it soon. It turned out to be a chunk of dried-up cow dung!

PRANKS AND PROWLS OF THE MARSH HAWK

Such surprises are typical if you observe the Northern Harrier. It is easily the most active hawk, much more so than the lofty Buteos that idle the hours away, perching or soaring in the blue, far above all other living things. Harriers seem to love fun and excitement. They "capture" mock prey, play tag with crows or magpies, and mob deadly Peregrines as well as harmless birds such as flickers or Kestrels. Quartering the fields and meadows mile after mile, at low speed and low level, they encounter many other creatures, seldom resisting a squabble or threatening pass, even if the target is far too large an item for their modest menu.

One juvenile Harrier actually struck a jack rabbit weighing at least six times as much as its attacker. The reckless bird was shaken off quickly while its "prey" loped away. But the Harrier overtook it, landed in front and barred its way with spread wings. The big hare halted in bewilderment. Impossible situations like that can best be dealt with by ignoring them, or so the hare seemed to think. It resumed nibbling as if the bothersome bird did not exist, and eventually the Harrier flew away.

When a Harrier stands on the ground or a post, the diagnostic white crescent on the base of the tail is covered by the folded wings, making identification more difficult than while in flight.

Northern Harrier

Another jack rabbit, about half-grown, was not so lucky. Harassed by a Harrier, it dodged to and fro until a Swainson's Hawk streaked down from the sky and seized it at its second swoop. After a brief struggle, the hawk began to feed while the Harrier waited patiently for its turn.

Although it catches baby rabbits, pocket gophers or ground squirrels whenever it can, the Harrier's staple fare is much smaller: mice or voles. Their abundance is of critical importance to the hawks' family life. Every three or four years or so, the prolific meadow vole multiplies to densities that can exceed four hundred per acre, when the high-strung little rodents swarm over the countryside. But the following spring there may be no more than two or three where there were hundreds or even thousands before.

THE MORE THE BETTER

If their prey is at the top of a population cycle, the winged hunters raise large families. In such times of plenty, the male Harrier may become a swaggering bigamist, mating with two, sometimes even three or four females. Biologist Frances Hamerstrom, who studied Harriers for 25 years, discovered six cases of bigamy and three of "trigamy" in a high vole year when she found 34 active nests in her Wisconsin study area. In poor vole years, there might be only two or three breeding pairs. To verify the identity of her birds, Hamerstrom captured, tagged and color-marked more than 90 adult Harriers of both sexes. Another of her discoveries was the absence of pair fidelity among the breeding population from one year to the next.

Adult male Harriers can be easily identified from their brown mates by their light-gray color. The gull-gray wings of the male have black primaries, or flight feathers, as if they have been dipped in ink. The oldest males, which can attain an age of 16 years, are almost white on the belly. Why the sexes look so strikingly different from each other, as opposed to most other hawk species with similar looking sexes, is a matter of conjecture. No doubt, the dull brown plumage of the

Preceding page: The brownish iris of a juvenile hawk turns to yellow with maturity. At any age, the eyes of male Harriers are lighter in color than in females.

Harriers sleep on the ground, well-hidden in marshy vegetation. Particularly during winter, they may congregate at communal roosts, arriving from various directions around sundown.

Northern Harriers have been timed at 38 mph, but they usually fly much slower, using a combination of flapping and gliding.

female Harrier enhances her camouflage while brooding on her ground nest. Conversely, like gulls, the male's white underside makes him less conspicuous when seen against the sky, sailing low over the ground, seeking prey.

A little smaller and more slender than their mates, male Harriers are real show-offs that do not want to hide their presence from their own kind, particularly when it comes to attracting mates. Soon after arrival on their nesting grounds, even before winter snow has melted, the adult males perform amazing stunts—the so-called sky-dance, a series of steep U-shaped dives and ascensions, wings flapping all the while. At the zenith of his ascent, the bird flips over on his back, calling in a staccato cackle.

When the living is easy, females and immature males, still in their brown

Northern Harrier

juvenal plumage, do some sky-dancing as well. Later, both sexes collect building material for the nest, carrying long reed stems or twigs to a marshy spot, usually well-hidden in winter-ravaged cattails. In drier habitats, Harriers may choose a nest site among low buck brush or sage. In fat years, the females lay large clutches of six or seven whitish eggs that hatch after 30-32 days.

During their first week or so, the young are very dependent upon their mother for cover in wet weather, or shade from the midday sun. But very soon they wander away from the center of the nest, and from each other, to seek shelter in the surrounding vegetation. Seemingly quite fearless, a young Harrier hisses menacingly when you chance upon it. Facing the giant intruder, it will lean back on its tail and present its extended feet, armed with needle-sharp talons.

Although they are best left alone, Harrier nests can be located by watching the adults in another famous aerial show, the transfer of food. At the arrival of the male, the female rises from the eggs or small chicks, eagerly meeting her provider. When they are aligned in the right position, she flying just behind and below him, he drops the prey and she snatches the item from mid-air in a trick almost too quick to see, a marvelous example of the Harrier's dexterity. The female lands at once, either to take a bite herself or to feed the chicks.

After about five weeks, the male youngsters are the first to be on the wing, getting a head start on their bigger and often aggressive sisters. Up to the next spring, the juveniles can be recognized by the rufous color on chest and belly. Both sexes sport the tell-tale white crescent on the base of the tail. Its function may be obscure but likely has to do with visibility in twilight conditions. Harriers are active until late evening, when they often hassle their competitor and close neighbor, the Short-eared Owl, that rises from its daytime roost to begin the night-shift.

TAKEN BY SURPRISE

What do Harriers eat if their staple prey, the meadow vole, is scarce? Foregoing the sky-dance, many birds become nomads, traveling far and wide in search of greener pastures. Those that remain on their traditional nesting ground turn their predatory eye to other kinds of food, particularly birds. It is then that we

Northern Harrier

may see what this versatile hawk can really do.

Young shorebirds as well as ground-nesting passerines are always vulnerable to this slow and systematic predator. But adult male Harriers have a way of specializing in avian prey. Abandoning his characteristically slow quartering, he adopts a fast coursing flight, intended to surprise sparrows and larks, particularly at dusk. Sprinting among reedbeds, he scatters sandpipers and snipes like leaves in a storm. In spring, migrating shorebirds and snowbuntings, that locally congregate in large flocks on fields and meadows, are spied upon from a distance. The Harrier approaches at astounding speed, hugging the ground, his cupped wings beating below the horizontal, their tips not rising above the bird's back. In the final moment, with luck, he may seize the flushing prey in an astonishing burst of speed coupled with wing-thrashing agility.

Unfortunately for him, if successful, the male frequently loses his hard-earned booty again to a big female or hungry yearling, less skillful at hunting but persistent at piracy. In their open habitat, Harriers cannot hide from the envious eyes of other raptors either. Even the Peregrine is not above robbing the industrious mouser, and the big Buteos are among the worst of pirates.

In one exceptional case, an adult male Harrier retained his freshly killed prey despite a Red-tail's thievish intentions. In a spectacular ground-hugging attack, the Harrier had caught a Pectoral Sandpiper and landed in the grass. At the approach of the bigger hawk, the Harrier flushed well ahead, leaving his prey in the long grass. But the Red-tail failed to find it. After searching and circling for minutes, it gave up and left. Presently, the Harrier returned to his stashed prey and began to feed. Such incidents illustrate the unerring ability of Harriers to remember the exact location where they have left their prey, even on grassy meadows that to us seem quite featureless.

ALIVE OR DEAD

Less adept at capturing the shifty shorebirds and small passerines, female Harriers kill the occasional partridge, pheasant or duck, sometimes after a long and messy struggle. Lacking the powerful feet of a Goshawk or the killing bite of a falcon, she may begin to pluck her victim alive. Sensing the danger, mixed congregations of

When hunting, the Northern Harrier flies low over the ground
and drops quickly on mice or other birds in the grass.

waders and ducks rise at her approach, to move out of harm's way. She seldom presses them in extended pursuit, but instead suddenly seizes a teal or other small duck by surprise. Holding it by the head, she drags it up the shore. Rails and coots, especially the young, are often targeted. Once I saw a female Harrier pounce on a coot swimming in a narrow ditch. She sank up to her belly in the water but held on. Seconds later, the coot's mate arrived, rushing the Harrier in a thrashing fury of black wings and foaming water, forcing her to let go.

During years when botulism epidemics waste thousands of prairie waterfowl, Harriers collect along the shores of lakes and sloughs to feast, delaying their migration until well into fall. When freeze-up comes, adults and immatures vacate their vast northern breeding grounds and travel far south of summer range, to the delight of local hawk watchers who now have an opportunity to enjoy this elegant and entertaining marauder of the northern marsh.

Sharp—shinned Hawk

It is a brilliant winter's day and house sparrows have been thrilling in the back-yard all morning. Suddenly we become aware that a silence has set in. A casual glance outside reveals that the bird feeder is well-supplied but there is not a single feathered customer in sight. Then our eyes fall upon a still figure perched on a branch by the fence. Quite nondescript of color, gaunt and grim looking, it is clearly a hawk. In a rush of excitement, we grab the binoculars that are always within reach on the kitchen table.

Focusing hurriedly, we note that the hawk's head is small and blunt, almost reptilian, and its eyes are bright-red, glaring with near-insane intensity. Following their piercing gaze, we discover a sparrow clamped onto the base of the tree, like an outgrowth of the rough bark. Frozen with fear, the desperate bird is hidden from view by the trunk. But maybe others will not be so lucky.

Spreading its wings, the hawk drops lightly down behind a lilac bush. When it walks back into view, it drags a sparrow along in its clutches. After flying to a spruce tree farther back from the house, it begins to pluck. Puffs of feathers are drifting down to the ground. When a neighbor walks by on the other side of the fence, the hawk looks about warily and takes off, carrying its prey and disappearing between the houses.

Fascinated by the savage little drama that took place in our yard, we consult a bird guide and compare the pictures. What kind of hawk was it? After much deliberation, based on its shape, plumage and color, we decide that it must have been a Sharp-shinned Hawk. During the next few days, the birds at the feeder flush at the least sign of danger, real or imagined, rushing headlong into dense shrubbery. We often look outside, but never see the red-eyed raider again.

A STUDY IN STEALTH

Such sudden attacks, striking a terror in small birds, are typical of the smallest Accipiter, the Sharp-shin. A forest hunter by nature, it makes its feisty forays nearly anywhere in North America where there are a few bushes and trees to conceal its affairs—in rural settings, city parks, as well as remote wilderness. By

A Sharp-shin's legs are three-quarters bare, hence its odd name.

Sharp-shinned Hawk

and large, its breeding range stretches across the northern half of the continent, but its migratory wanderings extend down into the entire southern half, well into Central America. Raised in remote wilderness, northern migrants, especially the young, are not afraid of people and may carry on their business under our nose, yet they often manage to escape notice.

The Sharpie's inborn strategy is to approach unseen, hidden from its prey as well as from enemies such as crows that may call the alarm and give its presence away. Using the cover of trees and bushes, it operates by stealth and ambush. In hot pursuit of small passerines, it is deadly silent, streaking through trees and branches at breakneck speed. How good they really are at their craft can be appreciated if you see them perform under pressure.

Once I was standing below a nest of young Sharp-shins when one of the adults arrived. Startled by the human presence, it dropped the small prey it was carrying and shot up almost vertically through the crown of the tree without hitting a branch. Another time, I surprised one at its meal in the corner of a tennis court. Fleeing, it slammed into the wire fence and fell to the ground, stunned. Just as I bent down to pick it up, it jumped to its feet and took off, hitting the fence again on the other side of the court. One of its claws caught in the wire and the bird hung upside down for a few seconds before sliding to the ground like a wet towel. But it sprang to life once more and this time it took off parallel to the fence, disappearing into the dense brush surrounding the court. The branches were so tightly interlaced that one would have thought it impossible for a medium-sized bird to pass through, especially after having been subjected to a severe battering, yet the hawk made it without a hitch.

When hunting in the woods, the Sharp-shin flies from tree to tree. Darting across a trail or flitting through an opening, they are gone before one has time to focus the eye, like a shadow or a thought half-remembered. Was that a bird or just our imagination?

GUERILLA TACTICS

Fortunately, these secretive little guerrillas do some hunting in the open too, especially during migration times. One September day, when a heavy shower had just passed and a brilliant double rainbow arched over golden stubble

Tiny and delicate, but ferocious, the male Sharp-shin is just a little bigger than a robin. Almost twice the weight of her mate, the female is a little larger than a jay.

Young Sharp-shins are able to fly about 23 days after hatching.

Preceding page: Field identification of the Sharp-shinned Hawk can be difficult, even for experts. A good diagnostic point is the Sharpie's square-tipped tail.

Sharp-shinned Hawk

fields, a Sharp-shin alighted on a straw bale nearby. Through the field glasses, I could see every detail of its plumage, the long grab-ready toes, and the keen eyes, bright like the raindrops that glittered on every blade and sprig. The field was alive with small birds, Lapland Longspurs, migrants from the North, and the Sharp-shin was stalking them. In the final burst of speed, it dashed at the nearest ones, but when they flushed in time, the hawk gave up soon and settled back onto a bale.

After the longspurs had descended again to resume feeding, some distance away, the hawk flew low from bale to bale, attempting to get close enough for the next sprint. Half a dozen of its surprise attacks were foiled until one of the little birds tried to dodge by dropping back onto the ground. The Sharpie somersaulted and seized it in a flash. It sat on the ground awhile before carrying its booty to the nearest willow bushes.

GAMES OF CHANCE

An unusual hunting method they employ is a falconlike stoop, most often seen during migration seasons, when Sharp-shins travel and soar high in the sky. At the sight of small birds flying below them, they may suddenly forget their shy nature and zoom down in a hissing dive with wings pulled in. Such spectacular hunts often fail, but some prey are snatched out of the air after vigorous pursuit. One Sharpie fell like a stone from a great height into a feeding flock of snow buntings that rose with a roar of small wings. The hawk ate its kill in a weedy corner of a wide open field, far from the cover of trees.

Young Sharp-shins love to tease and harass birds too large to kill, such as crows, kestrels, kingfishers or flickers. Despite their loud protests, some of these species seem to suffer from a fatal weakness; time and again they return to their tormentor, even when perched quietly in a bush. When you watch these games, it seems obvious that both parties are enjoying themselves. Of course, for the hawk, it is a thin line that separates play from work. If the Sharpie could manage to hold on to one of its sturdy playmates, its instinctive urge to kill and eat would be activated quickly. It is this dominant evolutionary force that has kept the little rascal alive and prospering for millions of years, much longer than our own rapacious and successful species has walked upright and dominated the earth.

Cooper's Hawk

To the consternation of early European settlers, the forbidding forests of the New World contained many threats to life and livelihood. Not only wolves and bears, which were eventually driven out, but pernicious and persistent pests such as the birds of prey. The most ubiquitous was no doubt the Cooper's Hawk. Exactly in-between the two other Accipiters in weight and wingspan, the Cooper's combines some of the bold power of the Goshawk with the nimble sneakiness of the Sharpie. In size, it seems to have been designed especially to prey on young chickens. Imagine a homesteader's chagrin when the "Chicken Hawk" returned day after day, carrying away a prized leghorn before one had time to aim the musket.

Inspired by its looks as well as habits, another old-timers' nickname for the chicken hawk was "Blue Darter." Perhaps this colorful epithet should have been retained instead of today's prosaic Cooper's Hawk. The bird's official name honors zoologist William Cooper, who lived from 1798 to 1864 and first described this exclusively New World species.

As hawks go, the adult Cooper's is considered quite pretty. About the size of a crow, it is finely barred with a rusty color on the breast and belly, bluish-gray on the back, with a darker crown and ruby-red eyes. The older the hawk, the darker its iris. Young birds have yellowish eyes and brownish plumage, heavily streaked on breast and belly.

DUET IN THE DEEP WOODS

Silent during winter, the male Cooper's becomes quite vocal when he goes courting. In fact, he may be the only raptor that delights in serenading his partner during mating and nest building. Uttering a variety of repetitious clucks, the pair call to each other in early morning duets that can go on for an hour. Afterward, they copulate, and perhaps bathe in a forest pool and spend some time preening before hunting again.

Nest building is done mainly by the male while the female watches, occasionally chattering her approval or adding the finishing touch. He collects dead branches by breaking them off trees with his feet. Smaller twigs may be transported in the bill. Placed on horizontal branches against the trunk of a

The breeding range of the Cooper's Hawk includes all of the contiguous states and extends well up into Canada, except on the open plains.

Cooper's Hawk

conifer, or in a crotch of a dense deciduous tree, the nest is a little over two feet wide and quite flat-topped. The bowl, which will hold the three to six bluish eggs, is lined with flakes of bark, and from time to time the nest rim is decorated with green twigs.

During the early stages of incubation, the hawks are secretive. When you disturb them, they may remain hidden but protest in a staccato cacking that gets more emphatic as the season progresses. If there are young on the nest, some females become bold enough to approach the intruder with startling feints aimed at one's head.

Researchers who want to check the breeding success of this hawk have invented a trick that makes finding nests easier; they broadcast a taped version of the bird's calls. If they get within hearing range of a territorial pair, the female or male ventures forth to challenge the faked intruder, unwittingly leading researchers back to the nest.

THE LOYAL COUPLE

Nest fidelity among male Cooper's Hawks has been found to last for life. If he loses his mate, he tries to attract a new one by displaying in typically slow-beating, undulating flight over his home range. At one site in Alberta, a local "bird-lover," worried about losing too many robins and bluebirds to the hawks, boasted about shooting six females in succession. Every time the shy male escaped destruction and managed to attract a new mate in a matter of days. Until he too was shot.

Nowadays, such misguided persecution is against the law everywhere, which is a good thing, for the hawks have a difficult time as it is. Despite their protective and aggressive nature, they have enemies, particularly Great Horned Owls and raccoons, that may rob eggs or nestlings at night and even kill the brooding female.

In recent times, over much of its breeding range, the Cooper's Hawk has become quite rare as an indirect result of the use of agricultural pesticides, loss of habitat, and a declining prey base. Considered threatened or endangered, the future of the Blue Darter is in some doubt in many of the eastern states where it was once feared and hated as the all-too-common Chicken Hawk.

Besides robins, starlings, jays, quail, and a long list of other birds, the Cooper's Hawk often catches chipmunks and young rabbits.

Northern Goshawk

In bygone days, before the human race acquired the power to kill at a distance, birds of prey probably reacted to the bizarre biped with the same indifference or mild curiosity they still regard a pig, a deer or a Hereford bull. To find a hawk that still behaves toward humans in such a trusting way, you must go far north into the wilderness. Most likely, it will find you first.

Camping or fishing in boreal Canada or Alaska, going quietly about your business, you will sooner or later be checked out by the avian hunter of the northern forest. Searching for prey by sound as well as sight, it may have been alerted by a small noise you made. Approaching unseen in low flight, it swoops silently up to perch in a pine above you. Alerted by the click of claws on wood, you are a little startled to see it sit there, so close by, superior in its winged mobility, untouchable and aloof.

The hawk may never have seen a human being before. And you, in turn, marvel at this magnificent figure of martial perfection. Finely vermiculated with wavy lines on breast and belly, its color is gray and subdued, like misty woods. But there is nothing soft or fuzzy about its head: the bloodshot eyes glare at you, unblinking, under frowning brows. Secure in the knowledge that you are well outside its range of prey, a glance at its heavily armed feet hints graphically at the terrible fate of rabbit or grouse.

The full fury of an angry Goshawk can be experienced first-hand if you come too close to its nest. If it stops cacking, watch out! Approaching low and often from behind, it dashes at your head, zooming by only inches away. The best thing to do is to protect your face and get out of there. Wild animals such as foxes or even moose are probably evicted in the same unequivocal way. Interestingly, Goshawks that breed in densely populated regions behave quite differently. Having learned the range of a shotgun, they remain at some distance, calling vociferously, even if you climb the nest tree.

THE CYCLE OF LIFE AND DEATH

The occurrence of Goshawks in the northwoods varies from year to year and is closely tied to the population cycles of their major prey, snowshoe hares. Every

Goshawks are good at nest building, collecting sticks and twigs that they break off trees or gather on the ground. The chicks mature 5 to 6 weeks after hatching. They remain dependent upon the parents for food for a long time thereafter.

Northern Goshawk

ten years or so, the hares go from great scarcity to incredible multitudes, supplying avian and mammalian carnivores with a feast, and boosting the size of their families. After the rabbit population declines, as a result of starvation or disease superimposed on the growing impact of predation, the Goshawk shifts its attention to birds. In lean times it will chase a fleeing grouse tenaciously, veering and twisting between trees, perhaps passing right by you, oblivious to the human observer.

Such rare glimpses into the hunting life of this big woodland hawk always happen by sheer luck. One bitterly cold December day, near Lake Athabasca in Northern Canada, I was watching a covey of ptarmigan, resplendent in immaculate white, a delicate gleam of pink on their breast. The birds were quietly picking willow buds from branches sticking up out of the deep snow. Suddenly an adult Goshawk sailed down the hillside and seized one of the ptarmigan, point-blank, a few yards away from where I stood. Glaring at me, bold and bright in the cold light of the winter sun, it sat belly-deep in the fluffy snow. Then it flapped its wings, rose heavily and flew into the woods, white booty dangling.

Another time, while I was watching a Short-eared Owl pounce onto its prey in a grassy field, I was puzzled to see it rise in a hurry, drop its small prey, and begin to climb steeply. The reason quickly became apparent when a Goshawk entered my binocular view, flying in circles under the owl and trying to overtake it. Buoyant on its long wings, the Short-ear gained height as steeply as if it were ascending a staircase. The hawk gave up soon and sailed back to the woods from where it had come. Probably, it had hoped to get close to the owl while it was still on the ground, unaware of its peril.

SEARCH AND DESTROY

The Goshawk's most common foraging strategy is a synthesis of search and surprise. Flying from perch to perch, it patrols a creek bed or woodland edge, pausing at each stop, spying for squirrels, rabbits or birds. If it spots something of interest, it waits for the most opportune moment before launching its attack, rocking its head sideways to check out the distance. Living in an environment of vertical lines, Goshawks take their bearings from the trunks of standing

In western states such as Oregon, the breeding ranges of all three Accipiters can overlap and they have been found nesting as close as 300 to 500 yards apart, which comes at a grave risk for the smaller species—the Goshawk is not above raiding their broods.

Northern Goshawk

trees. In contrast, open-country raptors bob their heads up and down to measure an object's position relative to the flat horizon.

Goshawks are versatile hunters that attack in an astounding burst of speed or a crafty sail that maximizes the element of surprise by clever use of terrain. However, while soaring over the woods or crossing a river, they do not hesitate to swoop down with flexed wings, like a falcon, if a crow or gull happens to pass under them. In wetlands, shorebirds and ducks are hunted by coursing low among the reedbeds. Adult Goshawks do not like to tackle heavy prey over water, but the young are not yet so smart. One migrating juvenile seized a duck over a prairie slough and, holding its prey, plunged into the water, which happened to be no more than chest-deep for the bird. After sitting still for several minutes, it managed to get airborne again and carried its quarry into shoreline woods.

THE BEAUTIFUL BARBARIAN THAT COMES IN FROM THE COLD

Young Goshawks raised in the wilderness begin migrating south in early autumn. Adults tend to stay north as long as possible, but in years when the boreal wilderness becomes barren of small game, they too may be forced to leave the breeding ranges. In so-called invasion years, hawks that come in from the cold may reach the latitude of Florida and Texas. Attracted by pigeons or chickens, some take up temporary residence near farms and country homes, returning each day, until the owners cannot help but notice their dwindling stock.

The adult male Goshawk can be very good at catching pigeons, which are among the fastest of birds. One male waited habitually in a high power pylon for flocks of pigeons to fly by along the edge of adjacent woods. At their distant approach, the Goshawk dipped down along a cutline, out of sight of the pigeons, flew fast across the woods and emerged at the other end into the open at the exact moment they were passing. Mounting steeply with momentum, the hawk grabbed a bird out of the flock before it had time to turn aside. Other adult males have demonstrated surprising endurance, pursuing pigeons in full flight and seizing them high in the sky, or forcing them down to the ground.

Preceding page: Eye color seems to function as a status symbol among Goshawks as well as all Accipiters; the older the bird, the deeper ruby-red its iris.

The Goshawk has white undertail coverts that are fluffed out prominently during display, in flight as well as on a perch.

Many a Goshawk will eventually pay for its raids on the pigeons by getting shot or being captured in a baited trap. Designed in Sweden, the lower portion of a commonly used hawk trap is a wire cage containing a live stool pigeon. The top portion includes heavy trap doors that fall shut if a predator enters and perches on the trigger. Deadly effective, these traps are a trade secret among rural pheasant farms and pigeon fanciers, who take an unknown toll on hawks and owls, legally or illegally.

Losses of Goshawks are particularly heavy among the year's juveniles—coupling the ignorance of mankind with the immature's lack of hunting skills. Well over two-thirds of the year's young can be expected to perish of starvation or accident during their first winter. Yet, by spring, enough of these innocents will return to the cold northwoods to carry on the age-old traditions of their barbaric, yet beautiful, race.

Red-shouldered Hawk

High over the canopy of budding hardwoods, alternating a few flaps with a glide, the circling Red-shouldered Hawk is the picture of artistry. As though burnished by the warm rays of the evening sun, its undersides flash the color of flame. Against the light, the white ellipses on wings and tail gleam like pearls on velvet.

"*Hey-you, hey-you,*" repeated over and over, its shrill, drawn-out cry is a cherished sound of spring to all who are familiar with this pretty, graceful Buteo. In pre-settlement days, its plaintive voice must have greeted aboriginal people everywhere in the riverine woodlands of eastern North America, from the Maritime provinces of Canada down to Florida and the Gulf Coast. Abundant and guileless, these soaring hawks did not have a compulsion for secrecy like other woodland raptors, such as the Accipiters.

After the arrival of Europeans, when the stately oaks, chestnuts, beeches and hemlock fell to the ax, one by one, the native Red-shoulders were driven from nest and home. The open mosaic of fields and woodlots better suited the Red-tail, which eventually replaced its smaller cousin in agricultural regions. This succession from one species of *Buteo* to another was already noted more than half a century ago by Arthur Cleveland Bent, author of the incomparable *Life Histories of North American Birds Of Prey* published in 1937.

Bent had been studying local hawks since 1882, and he knew of over 30 breeding pairs of Red-shoulders within fifteen miles of his Massachusetts home. Some of these sites were monitored over a span of 44 years, during which he inspected over 177 nests. The eggs of the Red-shoulder, Bent wrote, were the most handsome of all the Buteos' and came in a variety of colors and patterns.

Today, local populations of this medium-sized Buteo are recovering and thriving again. In some states, it has even adapted to nesting in suburbs. Curiously, there is also an isolated population of Red-shoulders in California that seems to be slowly expanding to the north and east.

RED OR NOT-SO-RED

Although ornithologists recognize five geographic races of Red-shoulders, the birds differ little in appearance and intergrade gradually. All of these supposed

The loss of riparian woodland has resulted in wide-spread declines of Red-shouldered Hawks in the Southeast, yet the species appears to be recovering, especially in Florida.

Red-shouldered Hawk

subspecies can be readily identified by their auburn, crescent-shaped wing panels and the conspicuous barring on wings and tail. Those in Florida are the palest and smallest, while those in California the deepest robin-red. Bent and his egg-collecting associates were so impressed with these western hawks, which were reported to be fond of Eucalyptus groves, that they gave them a separate name: Red-bellied Hawk.

The name did not stick, but recent studies in California have confirmed what Bent already knew, that Red-shoulders show a high degree of site continuity and pair fidelity, and that there is no lack of new partners if one of a pair is lost. A male captured for research, to be fitted with a radio-transmitter, was replaced by another male within two hours. When released again, the original resident lost no time to oust the intruder, which was found to be a so-called "floater" that ranged over the territories of eight breeding pairs, waiting for a vacancy to open up.

Partial to riparian woodlands, never far from a creek or beaver pond, the Red-shoulder builds its nest in the crotch of a large tree, usually deciduous, well below the canopy. Hidden from predatory eyes above and below, the platform is about two feet wide and one foot deep, constructed from fine twigs and branches. The rim is decorated with green sprigs of hemlock or cedar, which are refreshed almost daily, a habit the Red-shoulder shares with most other hawks. Its function is obscure but it may improve sanitation or help repel parasites.

THE FURTIVE FAMILY

Both sexes take turns incubating the two to four eggs, coming and going furtively and communicating in soft voices, guarding their sanctuary against enemies and intruders. After the eggs hatch, in about 33 days, a hectic period commences. The young will have to be fed 10 to 15 times a day for the next six to eight weeks.

Hunting quietly from a perch low in a tree, often on the edge of a pond or marshy area, the male supplies all the prey he can muster: frogs, garter snakes,

Preceding page: Snakes can be an important food item for the Red-shouldered Hawk.

In much of its breeding range, except the northern portion, Red-shouldered Hawks are residents year-round.

Red-shouldered Hawk

The Red-shouldered Hawk has a strong affinity for unbroken hardwoods,
and usually nests not far from water.

tiny turtles, mice, chipmunks, as well as a few birds. Delivering his catch to the
female, she tenderly feeds the young, bite for bite, until they can tear up the prey
themselves or become too impatient to wait, seizing it the instant she lands.
Spurred on by their chirping hunger calls, the male seldom dawdles. Before long,
she joins him in foraging to meet the insatiable demand.

Without having been shown why or how, the chicks know instinctively what they have to do to keep their home clean. Awkwardly crawling at first, and later carefully stepping backward, they approach the edge of the nest to eject their excrement over the rim. Soon, the area around the base of the tree becomes sprinkled with white-wash, a sure sign to human visitors that the nest is occupied. As additional evidence, a lot of fluffy down sticks to the edge and surrounding branches.

Sleeping or resting most of their early days, the chicks become more active and spend a lot of time preening once their feathers begin to grow. After about two weeks, pin feathers emerge from the same papillae (shaft) as the second coat of down, pushing it out until it drops off, transforming the furry-looking chicks into more normal-looking birds. The flight feathers sprout first, followed by the feathers that cover the wings. The back is fully feathered before the sides and the breast. Thighs and head are last to be filled out.

Keen-eyed, the maturing youngsters watch anything that moves or flies by, twisting their heads comically to catch a glimpse of a swallow overhead, or to follow the erratic passing of a butterfly. Exercising in spells, they flap their wings vigorously, holding steady by gripping the branches firmly with their feet. After about five weeks, they venture out onto adjoining tree limbs and become "branchers."

At this time, a few wispy remnants of fluff still stick to head and body, making them look clownish and harmless, deceptively masking their quick temperament. If approached or handled by a human, they hiss fiercely, ready to slash with razor-sharp claws that can draw blood in an instant.

The great moment when the first youngster becomes airborne arrives quite suddenly. Sooner or later it is followed by its siblings. The woods ring with their belligerent squabbles, each youngster out for itself, jealously mantling over every morsel that they manage to snatch from their parents or each other.

It will take another three weeks or so before they begin to behave like hawks, independent and self-contained. Circling upward over the canopy of their home woods, tails fanned, wings beating in short bursts, they do what comes naturally to their kind. Screaming an ageless challenge, they set their sights on the horizon, free as the wind.

Red-tailed Hawk

Spring has arrived on the northern plains, but the day has been raw and wet. On a fence post out in the open, forlorn, leaning into the frigid wind, sits a Red-tailed Hawk. At long intervals, it flutters down to the grass and picks up something in its bill, perhaps a small frog or earth worm.

Returning to a post, it resumes its desolate watch, until it flies listlessly out over the pasture. Halting, it hovers against the wind for a few moments, some twenty feet up, then plunges down. Just before it reaches the ground, a small bird flushes under it, their outlines merging, or so I thought.

Watching through binoculars from some distance away, I could just see the hawk, partly hidden in the grass. Its movements indicated that it was feeding, but I was puzzled by the length of time it took to finish prey the size of a small bird. When the Red-tail finally flew off, about 25 minutes later, I walked toward the spot where it had been, hoping to collect some remains by which to identify its kill. Instead of the feathers of a lark or sparrow, I found the bloody carcass of a duck! Partially consumed, trailing a wind vane of plucked down, the female pintail lay three feet from her nest with eggs.

The above observation illustrates the pitfalls of interpreting hawk behavior in the field. The capture or near-miss of prey happens so quickly that it is easy to draw false conclusions. Secondly, the incident demonstrates that there is more to the Red-tail than meets the eye. It is generally considered a harmless or even beneficial raptor that kills mainly rodents. Particularly during lean times, it is an active member of the sanitation brigade that cleans up carcasses of animals that died of a variety of causes, including contagious diseases. But close observation reveals that it is also a versatile hunter with a nondiscriminating taste, varying from small mammals to invertebrates, from birds to snakes, from amphibians to fish.

BY HOOK OR BY CROOK

The depredation of this common and most widespread hawk has been the subject of much debate and hundreds of scientific papers. Back in 1893, study methods were harsh but unequivocal. Researchers simply examined the

The Red-tail's breeding range spans the continent. The color of the upper tail makes adults easy to recognize. However, immatures lack the rufous and can be tricky to identify in the field.

Red-tailed Hawk

digestive tract of birds that had been shot. About half of 562 stomachs contained mice and less than 10% game birds or poultry.

More recent methods used to evaluate the diet of Red-tails center on the careful collection of pellets under roost trees. Regurgitated by the hawks from time to time, pellets contain indigestible food remains that can be identified and counted. Substantial lists have also been compiled from items found near nests. For ease of observation, some researchers did not hesitate to take the young hawks out of the nest and tether them at the base of the tree, where the parent birds continued to feed them.

Most studies reported that small mammals constituted 60 to 80 percent of the number and biomass of the Red-tail's food, in winter as well as summer. In addition, the hawks consumed a wide spectrum of non-mammals, including many birds. The unknown factor, frequently cited by the researchers, was that they could not tell whether species such as ducks, pheasants or songbirds had actually been captured by the hawk or scavenged.

Noted biologist Paul Errington, who conducted his innovative and exhaustive field research on predator and prey relationships in Wisconsin during the mid 1900s, considered the Red-tail "an awkward Buteo whose food habits were largely a function of prey conspicuousness and availability." In other words, what it sees is what it gets. Like most predators, it is an opportunist that eats anything it can catch, by hook or by crook.

Slow but big, the Red-tail is an unabashed bully and kleptomaniac that keeps an envious eye on other Buteos, Harriers, Accipiters or falcons. Any smaller raptor that does not carry its catch away quickly runs the risk of losing it to the Red-tail. If the Peregrine Falcon, supreme aerial hunter, brings down a duck too heavy to transport, the Red-tail will attempt to chase the falcon off, or it waits for a share of the left-overs. Only big female Peregrines are able to stand up to hungry Red-tails.

Preceding page: Red-tail chicks are sometimes preyed upon by owls or other hawks that may nest in the same woods. Less sudden but just as deadly are infestations of parasites and insects.

As raptorial birds go, the Red-tail is a long-lived species that has been known to survive in the wild for twenty-one years. Only eagles and vultures live longer.

Red-tailed Hawk

Unwittingly, a Peregrine sometimes creates an opportunity for other hawks to obtain prey that is normally too fast or alert. One spring day, a Red-tail sailed down and seized a Marbled Godwit crouched in the grass, its eyes glued warily on a soaring Peregrine. It probably never saw the danger coming up from behind. Godwits are among the wariest and speediest of shorebirds and are very seldom taken by any raptor.

For brute force, the Red-tail meets more than its match in the eagle, which will not hesitate to rob a prey-laden hawk of a freshly caught rat or rabbit. Relations between the powerful Goshawk and the big Buteo are stand-offish. But the Red-tail's most dangerous nemesis is the Great Horned Owl, a close but treacherous neighbor that may raid the hawk's nest at night and carry off the young to feed its own. During hard times, it may even tackle an adult Red-tail.

Rivalry and competition between these two species, the owl and the hawk, are severe, for food as well as home sites. Owls breed earlier than hawks. Unable to build their own nest, they usurp any existing nest that is large enough to accommodate them. In the northwoods, Red-tails that have been away on migration often find last-year's place taken, forcing them to construct a new nest, usually not far away.

No Place Like Home

For northern hawk watchers, the return of the Red-tail is a red letter day. When you approach the winter-ravaged nesting site, it is a thrill to hear the hawk's garrulous cry and spot it soaring over the trees. It shows great fidelity to territory and mates, nesting in the same woodlot year after year. If one of the pair is late in arriving, a new partner may be attracted soon, to be evicted just as quickly when last year's occupant arrives. Fights for nest sites are fast and furious, but settled soon. The northern Red-tail loses little time setting up house-keeping, giving its progeny the maximum number of days to become independent before the short summer ends.

During courtship, the pair displays in undulating flight, alternately swooping down and zooming upward, tilting over majestically for the next roller coaster dive. As a prelude to copulation, they often fly with feet dangling, calling to each other. During inactive periods, they stand sentinel on a tall snag, advertising their presence to one and all, their white breasts gleaming in the spring sun, visible from afar.

Some individuals can be recognized by color differences that range from almost black to nearly white. The great variety in plumage of this wide-spread species has given rise to much discussion about sub-specific status. Officially, the American Ornithologists' Union (AOU) recognizes five different races of Red-tails in North America: Eastern, Western, Fuertes', Harlan's, and Krider's. The Harlan's breeds in Alaska and is very dark in color. The Krider's occurs on the northern Great Plains and is mostly white. However, there are intermediates between all of these races, and dark and light variations can occur anywhere, between breeding pairs as well as among siblings.

To complicate matters even more, the rufous tail, that makes recognizing adults so very easy, is not always present. Harlan's and Krider's have whitish tails that may be mottled or finely barred with light brown. And the upper tails of immatures of all races are finely barred with gray-brown, showing no red at all.

Red-tails that lack the rufous badge of distinction are hard to recognize, particularly dark variants that resemble the darker form of three other Buteos: the Rough-legged, Swainson's, and Ferruginous Hawk. At a distance, they may be impossible to tell apart, even for expert hawk watchers. We will have to let them go as UFB's: Unidentified Flying Buteos.

Swainson's Hawk

Like trout in a stream, a dozen Buteos ride the strong Chinook wind gusting up the Rocky Mountain foothills that are fresh with the delicate green of early spring. From time to time, one of the hawks furls its wings, tilts over and swoops down to the base of the slope, leveling off low over the uneven soil pockmarked with "gopher" mounds. Scores of ground squirrels are gamboling in the grass, unaware of the danger overhead, yet the hawks miss time and again.

Sailing back up, they resume their place over the hill, riding the unruly updraft that lifts their bodies as well as their spirits. Some hawks make playful passes at each other or pick up mock-prey such as clods of clay that shatter on impact when dropped. One bird releases a harder object, perhaps a stone, that ricochets down the slope and is recaptured as if it were prey. When the hawk drops the item again, another one swoops and catches the plummeting pebble in mid-air.

Twice, a hawk swoops at a small bird, a lark or sparrow, that flushes from the ground in the nick of time. Others gang up on a passing Golden Eagle that defends itself by rolling over on its back, presenting talons, deflecting the swoops of the pesky hawks.

It is a spring scene common to all western hills where ground squirrels abound, turning grass into meat, and supplying the mainstay for a host of predators, mammals as well as birds. Soon after the rodents emerge from hibernation, hawks, eagles and Prairie Falcons congregate to have a feast. Last year's young, not yet ready to mate and raise a brood, have lots of time for play, with their own kind as well as other species. Local hotspots provide an opportunity to test our skill at field identification of adults and immatures, and to compare the Red-tail with the less common Swainson's Hawk.

GOPHER HUNTER PAR EXCELLENCE

Named a decade ago after English zoologist William Swainson, a better label for this typical prairie Buteo would have been "Gopher Hawk." Not as bulky as the Red-tail, it has narrower wings that have only three notched primaries

Swainson's Hawks react anxiously to humans and have been known to desert their nests after only one visit. At other times, they can be very "tame," letting cars and people pass by their perch a dozen paces away.

Swainson's Hawk

instead of four, making the tips look more pointed. Also, when soaring, it holds its rigid wings uptilted at a slight angle. (As a field mark, wing shape is diagnostic for adults as well as immatures, including the rare dark form.) In typical plumage, the hawk's light underwing linings help to identify it in flight. While perched, the adult's dark bib contrasts with the Red-tail's white chest.

Where their ranges overlap, both Buteos take the same kind of prey, and both are equally deadly when hunting ground squirrels. The final strike can occur after a low approach or a terrific stoop from the sky. Ground squirrels are very muscular and can deliver a nasty bite to the captor's feet. Unless the hawk is hungry, it may sit for awhile, just holding the prey until it expires. One Swainson's carried its catch to a fence post and waited close to an hour before beginning to eat. The poor "gopher" escaped or was released twice, dropping to the ground and running away. But it was recaptured in an instant.

Gophers are considered pests and are controlled by farmers and ranchers with strychnine-treated grain, which may have lethal repercussions for predators and scavengers that consume the poisoned rodents. Fortunately, Swainson's and Red-tails usually disembowel their prey, discarding the entrails in which the strychnine is concentrated.

Despite its preference for rodents, the Swainson's is surprisingly handy at hunting birds, always ready to swoop at larks or sparrows scurrying on the ground, failing to heed the soaring hawk. Some pairs feed their young a high proportion of avian prey, particularly fledglings of ground-nesting species. One blustery day, an adult Swainson's hovered over a prairie slough and swooped down into the weed-infested water. Pecking at its catch, the hawk began to sink slowly down to its belly. After some minutes, it rose, carrying a bird. Wading knee-deep to the spot where the strike had taken place, I discovered a few tell-tale feathers of a Sora, a secretive bird of reedy marshes.

Yet, despite their prowess as hunters of mammals and birds, during late summer Swainson's Hawks are content to eat little but insects, especially grasshoppers, which are pursued on foot or in hop-scotch fashion. There is some speculation as to the Swainson's foraging habits during migration. Some think that the hawks eat very little during their journey down the continent, subsisting on stored body fat for long periods. Others report flocks of Swainson's feeding on insects in fields and pastures along the way.

The female Swainson's Hawk does nearly all of the brooding and feeding of the young, while the male supplies her with a wide-ranging menu.

Swainson's Hawk

While soaring, Swainson's Hawks hold their wings in a dihedral, and their tips are narrower than in other Buteos. Both characteristics are diagnostic for field identification.

DOWN THE CONTINENTS

Practically the entire North American population of this species makes an annual round-trip to Argentinean Pampas, a distance that may exceed 14,000 miles for some of the birds! The southward stream of migrants thickens toward

Preceding page: During migration, Swainson's Hawks can subsist on grasshoppers, yet they are capable hunters of mammals and birds.

Mexico, funneling down to the Isthmus of Panama, where their numbers become truly spectacular. Soaring over and under each other, often in opposite directions, hawks are difficult to count, but a photograph of a single kettle may contain six or seven hundred tiny specks.

These so-called "kettles" of hawks are not flocks in the usual sense, and differ from the flight formations of shorebirds, waterfowl, or blackbirds, which demonstrate tight unison and organization, based on each bird's need to be part of the group. By contrast, the mass gathering of hawks is entirely by circumstance. Although they involuntarily lead each other on to the next thermal, simply by using it, each hawk moves as an individual, arriving as a single and departing as a single. Upon entering the kettle from below and circling up, some turn left, others to the right. At the top of the column, as soon as they stop feeling lift, each sails away without looking back, following the line of least resistance.

Returning the same way, and spreading out from Central America across their vast northern breeding grounds, a few go as far as the sub-arctic tundra in Alaska. But the vast majority find summer homes on the interior plains, from Mexico and Texas up to the Canadian prairie provinces. Choosing open or semi-open habitats, an isolated tree or even a power pole will do as a base for the Swainson's bulky nest.

At your approach, the anxious owners will meet you from afar, calling plaintively. They may even desert the place after one intrusion, especially during the early stages of the breeding season. At other times, they are far from shy, perching on fence posts right by the road, or closely following a farm plow to pounce on rodents disturbed in its wake.

In recent decades, while much of the former prairie has been cultivated, the Swainson's has lost a lot of ground and is believed to be far less common than before. Here and there, it has adapted to agricultural land and even to urban sprawl in some western cities. Good foraging opportunities may be spotty, though, and some breeding pairs have been found to travel as far as 15 miles between nest and hunting range.

By contrast, the growth of woodlots and farm shelter belts on formerly open prairie has benefited the Red-tailed Hawk, which may be well-established by the time the "Gopher Hawk" arrives from its long transcontinental journey. In the relentless conflict and competition between the two cousins, the former's gain usually leads to the latter's loss.

Rough-legged Hawk

Worldwide, the genus *Buteo* has about two dozen species, each with a fairly restricted range that may be shared by more than one species. The exception is the Rough-legged Hawk, which is the lone representative of its clan around the entire top of the globe. As a breeding bird, it occurs on the circumpolar tundra from Labrador to Alaska, from Siberia to Norway.

In the Canadian barren lands, trees grow farthest north on sun-facing slopes along rivers flowing to the Arctic Ocean. In such sheltered valleys, the Rough-leg may nest in spruce, but in the remainder of the treeless tundra it has to choose a niche on a cliff or cutbank. The best ledges are overhung, giving protection from the weather as well as from mammalian predators. For such cozy retreats there is no shortage of occupants among other northerners, such as the Gyrfalcon, raven, and Golden Eagle. Since these hardy customers are on-site early, or even stay around all year, the first-choice is theirs and the Rough-leg has to make do with inferior locations.

With branches scarce, the nest is mostly constructed from willow twigs and any debris the hawks can carry, even the odd bone or caribou antler. The bowl is lined with grass and sedges. Refurbishing the place year after year, some traditional nests grow to a respectable bulk of three feet wide and several feet deep.

A few days before she lays her eggs, the female becomes lethargic, sleeping most of the time with feathers fluffed, and flying only when necessary with labored wingbeats. After the start of incubation, she continues to doze, saving her energy, but rises frequently to turn the eggs. Turning is especially vital at the beginning of brooding to prevent the egg membrane from sticking to the shell. Turning also spreads her body heat more evenly among the eggs. The procedure is accompanied by a deliberate ritual; standing up, she peers intently at her treasures and sweeps her bill gently between them, pushing the eggs toward her belly. When moving around, she holds her feet in a fist, the rear toe folded forward between the front toes which are bunched together, so that the deadly claws are out of harm's way.

As hatching nears, the chicks can be heard tapping and scraping inside the shell. She appears to listen intently, and applies less pressure to the eggs, reluctant to leave even if her attentive mate arrives with food. When the great

Compared to its large body size, the Rough-legged Hawk has a small beak and tiny feet. It often perches on stumps, treetops or the wires of power lines.

Rough-legged Hawk

moment comes and the chicks emerge, they lie limp and exhausted, too weak even to raise their heads.

The number of eggs and surviving young will depend on weather conditions and food supply. Even more than in temperate zones, rodent populations at these high latitudes are erratic. The life cycle of the arctic lemming, the hawk's mainstay, goes from boom to bust every three or four years. For Rough-legs and other predators, the living is easy in high lemming years, allowing them to raise large broods. Conversely, scarcity of rodents forces them to look for other fare, such as Ptarmigan, small song birds, or baby hares. Even the weasel may fall prey to the hawk when the larder is empty.

THE LONE TRAVELER

In their turn, food supplies and breeding success will have a bearing on the number and timing of the Rough-legs that will show up in their winter quarters. Departing their temporary summer home at the dictates of polar storms, adults and juveniles drift south by late September or early October, each on their own. Soaring and sailing in favorable weather, or steadily winging their way, they are unafraid to cross wide expanses of open water. Upon leaving the barrens, the hawks have to fly over a wide swath of boreal forest. Here and there, an open bog, mountainside or lakeshore provides a stop along the way.

If the hawks are hungry, they will readily accept a chance at carrion, be it a wolf-killed moose or any other dead animal, including baits set by trappers for fur-bearing animals. Guided by the tell-tale activity of ravens and magpies, the hawks descend between the trees. Some end up in the trap, to be dispatched and discarded as "trash" by the disgruntled trapper.

Once they get past the boreal belt, the Rough-legs should feel more at home on the fields and pastures of settled regions. Some continue their travels down the continent as far as Texas, others go no farther than necessary, eking out a living on the snow-covered plains.

The Rough-legged's legs, or tarsi, are feathered down to the feet, but this diagnostic feature is difficult to check under field conditions.

Rough-legged Hawk

The Rough-legged Hawk spends winter days out in the open.

Preceding page: The Rough-leg likes open country, but may choose a night roost in a spruce thicket.

WINTER SENTINEL

On winter territory, the Rough-leg retains its partiality for wide-open terrain and likes to sit on posts or stones. Choosing to perch on a tree, it seems clumsy, flapping for balance on very thin twigs. The cold does not seem to bother it much, even the bleakest winter wind. Its lax plumage hangs loosely down over its legs, which are feathered to the toes. Compared to a Red-tail of about the same body weight and size, the Rough-leg's feet and claws are rather small. No doubt, this is a matter of economics; why carry the weight of big feet when small ones will do for prey that is usually tiny?

As a further adaptation to its nomadic way of life and the lack of trees on its breeding range, the Rough-leg has relatively longer wings than other Buteos. It is a master at hovering, a skill honed to perfection whenever the wind blows. Against the slightest breeze, a hunting Rough-leg can hold itself suspended for minutes on end, maintaining its station as steadily as if it were perched on a pinnacle of rock.

Although both Red-tails and Swainson's hover at times, persistent hovering, from one lofty look-out to the next, typifies the Rough-leg. Often, its legs dangle, but to see whether they are feathered to the toes, which is indicative for the species, is rarely possible. In flight, typical birds are easily told apart by the black belly, white base of the tail, and the dark thumb patch on the underwing near the carpal joint. However, dark variants are much more difficult to recognize, since they closely resemble black variety Red-tails.

Curiously, in some regions, Rough-legs use communal roosts to spend the night, usually in a dense stand of spruce trees in a rural park or cemetery. Arriving after sunset, more than a dozen birds may come together, spreading out over the countryside again at first light. On the hunting ground, in fields where food is abundant, they may congregate with their own kind as well as other open-country raptors.

Occasionally, Rough-legs take a few small birds, even a partridge or two, and they are not above robbing other hawks. They may even dispute prey ownership with the local bully, the Red-tail, winning a few and losing a few. But if the rodent stock is adequate, allowing the Rough-leg to fill its crop with a few each day, it is content. Waiting out winter, it soars into the clouds at the first hint of spring, ready to set the clock back again and return to the still-frozen north, its exclusive home on the top of the world.

Ferruginous Hawk

Compared to other Buteos that share its arid western range, the Ferruginous Hawk strikes an imperial pose on a craggy perch as well as in search of prey. Scouting prairie hills, it swoops down on furled wings and skims the contour of the slopes like a guided missile, sailing just over the grass, ready to pounce on any gopher or rabbit that crosses its path. Rising steeply into the wind, it careens over the crest of a butte and swoops down again to resume its low coursing flight over the badlands below. This is not the way of a Buteo. It is usually the way of the Golden Eagle.

Except for its handsome white and rusty plumage, the Ferruginous resembles its larger relative in other characteristics. Its hooked bill is strongly eagle-like, as are its legs which are feathered to the toes. With a wingspan of five feet and over four pounds in weight, it far surpasses all other Buteos in size. In recognition of its beauty and proud bearing, the scientists who decided upon its taxonomic label gave the species a Latin name of distinction: *Buteo regalis*, the regal hawk.

Perhaps it should have been classified as an eagle instead, considering that eagles are just oversized Buteos, and that both genera are members of the same family, Accipitridae. In fact, the continents of Europe, Asia and Africa include at least half a dozen species of eagle, some of them little larger than the average Buteo. By comparison, it seems odd that North America can only boast two, the Golden and the Bald.

IF IT LOOKS LIKE AN EAGLE
AND BEHAVES LIKE AN EAGLE . . .

Like eagles, the Ferruginous has a propensity to construct a traditional eyrie, a huge structure of interlacing sticks and branches. Some prefer to build on the ledge of a cliff or ravine. Others, lacking steep terrain in their home range, make do with an isolated tree, or even a haystack or the roof of a deserted barn. With the addition of more material each year, the structure may surpass four feet in width and height. The inside bowl is lined with strips of bark and often with dried horse or cow dung.

The large, powerful Ferruginous Hawk is fiercely defensive of its accessible nesting site, and is capable of driving away larger predators, including coyotes.

Ferruginous Hawk

Some pairs just choose a nesting spot on the ground, between boulders on an open hillside or on the rim of a prairie ravine. To any smaller hawk such an easily accessible site would be hard to defend against ground predators, particularly the ubiquitous coyote. But the Ferruginous does not hesitate to mount an effective attack.

One coyote, trotting along nose to ground, was hit by one of the hawks before it knew what happened. To deflect further blows, it jumped up into the air every time the hawks swooped. Scrambling for cover, it escaped by sidling into some bushes. Coyotes react in the same way when attacked by Golden Eagles. Toward humans, the hawks are shy around the nest and may desert it during the early stages of incubation, even after only one intrusion.

Well before egg laying begins, perhaps as a sign of occupancy or ownership, the hawks decorate their "castle" with some greenery: a sprig of spruce, a leafy willow branch, or even some stalks of alfalfa. Creamy white with brown blotches, the 3 to 8 eggs weigh about 2.8 ounces each, a little more than the biggest chicken egg. At hatching, the baby hawks check in at about 1.75 ounces, but if food supplies are plentiful, the young males attain about 2 pounds in five weeks, and the females half again as much.

To feed itself and raise its brood, the Ferruginous takes a wide choice of prey. Powerful enough to tackle a full-grown prairie hare (with the pair cooperating), it is usually content with smaller animals, including young rabbits, prairie dogs, ground squirrels, as well as mice, lizards, snakes, and a few open-country birds, including their nestlings.

A field biologist in Idaho, who closely watched a nesting pair over two seasons, saw a total of 808 attempts at prey capture. The hawks were successful in 129 hunts, nearly 17%. The most productive methods were active flight, either low or high, including some hovering. And the least successful in terms of prey capture was still-hunting from a perch. However, the latter method was used most often by the hawks, particularly during calm weather, and is no doubt the most energy efficient.

Preceding page: Ferruginous Hawks usually produce two to three chicks per brood.
In years when food is abundant, they can produce up to five.

Young Ferruginous Hawks remain in the nest for five to six weeks and go without water,
except during rains. On hot days they are shaded from the sun by the parents.

Ferruginous Hawk

If prey, such as a rabbit, was spotted from afar then hid in grass or bushes, the hawks might land and try to flush it out on foot. In general, they preferred to hunt over open ground or scarce vegetation where prey was more readily spotted than in sagebrush and other dense ground cover.

WHITE OR BLACK

The light-colored underside of the Ferruginous helps to hide its approach from potential prey. Seen against the sky, a white hawk is supposed to be more cryptic and should be harder to detect than a dark one. Why, then, is there a color variety that replaces the white body and underwings with chocolate brown? Dark variants are also quite common among other open country hawks. The reason, so speculated one scientist, may again have to do with hunting efficiency. Prey animals that have learned to avoid light-colored hawks may have trouble recognizing the dark bird, perhaps considering it a harmless crow or goose. This should make black-variety hawks more successful at approaching prey than their typical light-colored relatives. However, it remains to be proven whether this is true.

To confuse the issue further, consider the fact that some prey species also include darker individuals. The spotty occurrence of black ground squirrels begs the question of how that color should affect their vulnerability. Surely, a dark gopher would stand out starkly against dry grasses, rendering it more conspicuous and liable to be selected first by a raptor hunting by sight. Unless a hawk would treat such unusual critters with caution, perhaps misidentifying them as a mink or skunk, that are quite capable of a strong defense.

Large and conspicuous in open country, either light or dark, the Ferruginous has suffered much from direct and indirect persecution by humans, as well as from changes to its habitat. It has declined over much of its former range and is a candidate species for inclusion on the Threatened or Endangered Species List. In some of the 17 states and 3 Canadian provinces where it still occurs, conservationists try to boost the breeding population by placing artificial nest platforms in trees and on utility posts. It would be wonderful to see this regal hawk regain more of its former range, soaring over the fields and pastures of the West like a rare, colorful eagle.

The legs of the Ferruginous are feathered to the toes, in the same way as in the Rough-legged Hawk.

Broad-winged Hawk

Believed to be North America's most numerous hawk, with population estimates at over one million, the Broad-wing is less well known than other Buteos, for it is in plain view only during part of the year. Soaring down the continent by the thousands each autumn, its migrations are routinely observed through telescopes and binoculars by legions of hawk watchers, gazing in awe at the seasonal spectacle. But well before winter sets in, the entire population of Broad-wings vanishes down the narrowing flyway to and beyond Panama. Soon after their return journey in spring, they drop out of sight again under the canopy of woodlands and wilderness in the eastern half of the United States and across the Boreal region of Canada.

During courtship, the Broad-wing occasionally rises above the trees and advertises its presence. But if you do not know its voice, its whistled "*kill-eeee*" sounds more like a songbird than a hawk. Once the pair settles down to the serious business of raising a brood, it drops largely out of view again, never drawing undue attention to itself by preying on chickens or pigeons.

Along the woodland edge, the hunting male sits halfway up in the foliage, concealed, indolent, often content to feed on frogs and toads that are easy to locate during their springtime orgy of mass procreation. The constant din of their tremulous voices is suddenly silenced when the hawk sails low over the pool and pounces, splashing down into the shallows. Lifting its catch out of the water and taking it to a perch, the bird consumes the entire amphibian but discards the glutinous string of spawn.

RECLUSE OF THE NORTHWOODS

Near the nest, the Broad-wing is amazingly tolerant of visitors, even if you walk right up to the tree. In his classical *Life Histories*, Bent relates an anecdote involving bird artist James Audubon, whose helper climbed to the nest of a Broad-wing. When the brooding female refused to leave, he covered her with a handkerchief and carried her down to the ground. Removing the cloth, Audubon measured the bird and sketched its picture while it remained indifferent and docile.

Although Broad-winged Hawks gather by the thousands along migration routes, they become solitary and reclusive during the breeding season.

Broad-winged Hawk

After doing most of the nest building and incubating, the female also guards and feeds the young. Very small chicks spend most of their time sleeping. Their tiny heads just droop forward onto the floor of the nest. But after about two weeks, they can stand up and turn their heads backward, tucking it into their feathers, the way an adult does when sleeping. At that age, they also begin to nibble and tug at the carcasses of prey that are supplied by the male, but delivered to the nest by the female.

When the chicks are about half-grown, she helps forage, bringing in a wide range of food items, including frogs and toads, lizards, snakes, minnows, small mammals, and a few birds, often fledglings. In her absence, the male takes his prey directly to the nest. At one site in the Adirondacks, researcher P. F. Matray observed from a blind that four toads, delivered by the male, jumped right out of the nest again!

Soon after the end of the nesting season, parents and brood rise above the woods again, responding to the seasonal stirring of wanderlust. They begin their long journey south in August.

While soaring, the blunt wings and finely banded belly make the crow-sized Broad-wing look like a cross between an Accipiter and a Buteo. And if you are not familiar with this species, it can be hard to identify, until it wheels in good light. The short, fanned tail shows two or three alternating bands of white and black, which are wider than in the Red-shouldered Hawk.

Having thousands of miles to go, with few feeding stops along the way, the Broad-wing's strategy is geared toward minimum expenditure of energy. Each morning, before leaving the night's roost, the birds wait until the weather warms sufficiently to allow for the formation of thermals. Climbing in flapping flight, they tentatively feel their way. If one of them begins to soar, it is quickly joined by others, setting their sails and ascending the invisible circular stairway.

ALONE IN THE SOARING CROWD

Since the thermals drift and bend with the lateral flow of air, a tail wind into the general direction of travel boosts the birds' average speed. During adverse air flows, they will eventually have to tack across the wind to resume their original course.

Preceding page: Broad-winged Hawks build nests that are smaller than other Buteos'
and barely large enough to contain the two or three young.

The crow-sized Broad-winged Hawk usually hunts for squirrels, snakes, lizards, rodents, and its favorite dinner—frogs and toads.

While sailing from one thermal to the next, the birds angle their wing tips backward and narrow their tails to improve aerodynamic efficiency during the forward glide, striving to maintain speed and altitude until they feel rising air again. Thermals are so important to the Broad-wing that it is loath to cross any expanse of water, returning to land as soon as the air stagnates.

If weather conditions improve, the hawk may soar out over the lake again, but more likely it will adjust its flight direction and follow the shore. For this reason, the mass of travelers becomes concentrated in four separate flyways along and between the Great Lakes. Continuing down both sides of the Appalachian Chain and upon nearing the Gulf of Mexico, the route finally parallels the coast.

Along the way, the stream of birds narrows, but their passage is uneven and can be blocked by local rain storms and strong head winds. The longer the delay, and the greater the build-up of waiting birds, the thicker the flow when the weather clears and releases them all at once.

On exceptional days during October, up to 100,000 birds may pass over eastern Mexico or Panama in a spectacular parade of soaring kettles. One 35-mm photo frame, enlarged and carefully counted, contained 1,206 birds!

The birds eventually become separated from one another and end up as they started, in solitude. Antisocial and territorial on the foraging grounds, most hawks remain on their own until the changing amount of daylight stirs them anew, awakening the urge to travel, this time in reverse direction. Regular as the seasons, the migrations of hawks and other birds are a time-honored tradition, and all we can do is observe and enjoy.

Hawks of the Deep South

From North to South down the American continent, the number of raptor species increases ten-fold, from no more than three or four in the barrenlands of the subarctic, to well over 30 in the palm-fringed Florida glades and the saguaro deserts of Arizona and Texas. Evidently, most hawks like it hot.

In addition to northern birds of prey that migrate south in fall, the sunshine states are home to vultures, kites, and Caracaras, as well as seven unique Buteo-type hawks, which have their main breeding range in Mexico and farther south in the Americas. They come in a colorful variety of shapes and sizes, and have unusual and fascinating habits.

Harris' Hawks may produce two broods between January and December.

Hawks of the Deep South

The **Short-tailed Hawk** is a small, long-winged Buteo that is restricted to the lower half of Florida, where it frequents mixed woodland and savanna. Unlike any other Buteo, it is a persistent hunter of birds. Soaring or kiting motionless on the wind, wingtips upturned, head down, it spies for prey in a deliberate style all its own. Swooping down with impressive agility, it manages to capture birds ranging in size from warblers to doves, taking them by surprise, often in the canopy of trees or among shrubs.

Along the Mexican border, in parts of Texas, Arizona, New Mexico, and California, five Buteo-type raptors add excitement to the hawk-watcher's day afield. Perhaps one of the easiest to identify is the **Common Black Hawk**, a stocky, broad-winged bird of medium size with black wings and body and a black-and-white tail. It frequents aquatic habitats and feeds largely on frogs, fish, crabs, and reptiles. A still-hunter by preference, it sits quietly overlooking a creek or pond. It also wades into water on its rather long butter-yellow legs, seizing crayfish or other unwary creatures.

Hawks of the Deep South

The **Zone-tailed Hawk** resembles the Black Hawk in color and tail pattern, but it is larger and slimmer. In fact, it looks and behaves more like a Turkey Vulture, particularly since it holds its wings in a strong dihedral (at an angle from horizontal) while gliding along and rocking from side to side. An astute observer proposed the novel idea that the Zone-tail mimics the slow and harmless vulture, and actively seeks its company, as a strategy to get close to potential prey, be it bird, mammal or lizard. At the last moment, the hawk suddenly dashes to attack in a surprising burst of speed.

   The **White-tailed Hawk,** as its name suggests, should not be too difficult to identify in the field since few species of hawks have white tails. However, this one also has a white underside, and it comes in a confusing mix of subadult and immature plumages that are almost entirely dark. A rather large Buteo, frequenting the coastal Plains of Texas, it soars, glides and hovers gracefully with its pointed wings in a strong dihedral, reminiscent of the Swainson's Hawk. Like the latter, it follows the farm tractor to prey on disturbed mammals and insects. White-tails are also quick to congregate on the edge of prairie fires. Hovering in the smoke, they pounce on any small creature fleeing or disabled by the flames.

Hawks of the Deep South

The rather rare **Gray Hawk** is unusual in its own way. It used to be called the Mexican Goshawk. Somewhat smaller than a Red-shoulder, it is short-winged and long-tailed, resembling an Accipiter in looks and dashing behavior. It can be recognized by the white crescent on the base of its tail.

Sharing the lower Rio Grande valley with the previous species, the even rarer **Roadside Hawk** is a brownish Buteo-type raptor, the size of a Broad-wing, that likes to sit quietly on a post or overhead wire. Spying for prey, it glides down to seize insects, rodents or reptiles. Both the Gray Hawk and the Roadside Hawk, so scarce in the southern states, are common raptors in Mexico and beyond.

Hawks of the Deep South

By far the most colorful of these hawks is the **Harris' Hawk** or **Bay-winged Hawk**. The former name is in common use, and derived from Edward Harris, a friend of Audubon. However, "Bay-winged" is much more descriptive. The word "bay" has many different meanings in English, though in the case of this tri-colored hawk, the name is no doubt derived from the same definition as a bay horse—typically chestnut in color with some black.

About Harrier-size, this open-country hawk is unmistakable, with a reddish brown shoulder patch, underwing linings and leg feathers. The body is dark brown and the tail white-and-black. In active flight, it looks powerful and captures a wide range of prey, up to jack rabbits in size. Feeling at home in hot, dry grasslands and scrubby deserts, it nests early in the year, often in a saguaro or paloverde.

Often seen in small groups, the Bay-wing displays two absolutely unique behaviors; it often breeds as a trio, one female mating and copulating with two males, and all three sharing the tasks of nest building and raising the young. The threesome even hunts together and may be joined later by the fledged young. If one of the group spots a rabbit or other prey, dodging into a tangle of cacti and mesquite brush, all gather around. While one of them attempts to drive the prey out of cover, others are ready to intercept it if it attempts to escape.

Its cooperative and easy-going disposition makes this striking hawk a favorite with American falconers. Tolerant of people, if unmolested, the Bay-wing thrives in the outskirts of cities such as Tucson, Arizona, where its major hazard is electrocution on residential power lines. A very successful species, this hawk is common in South America as far down as Chile and central Argentina. We in North America should feel flattered and fortunate that this southern sun-worshipper graces at least a small portion of this great and varied continent.

Fast, smart and versatile, Red-shoulders are equally good at capturing lizards, small mammals and birds. Their long list of prey includes owls as well as smaller hawks.

EPILOGUE

awks are at the top of the food chain, inextricably linked to other living things by what they eat. From birds, mammals and fish down to insects and plants, each level is sustained by the ones below. If one level is polluted or diseased, for instance by chemicals used in agriculture, no matter how minute the dosage, the toxins become concentrated along the chain until they reach lethal potency. The health of the top predators becomes an indicator of the health of the entire ecosystem, and ultimately of mankind.

The pesticide era of the 1950s and 1960s gave us a clear warning of what can happen to the higher creatures in the chain if they consume contaminated foods. An early signal that the system was in trouble was the plight of several species of raptorial birds, particularly the Peregrine Falcon and the Bald Eagle. Their decline and failure to reproduce in settled regions of Europe and North America set alarm bells ringing before harmful effects of the insidious chemicals became obvious in humans. Fortunately, after the use of persistent pesticides was reduced, falcons and eagles have now recovered. Moreover, the struggle to save them from extinction has raised the status of raptorial birds among the general public.

The preservation of healthy populations of raptorial birds should be of interest to all people, especially to those who manage the land, such as ranchers, farmers and foresters. Hawks are important as a natural check on rodent numbers. They get rid of mice and ground squirrels free of charge, cleaner and easier than artificial methods of control. And all they ask in return, is to be left alone. In agricultural regions, the number of hawks can be

enhanced by leaving some breeding habitat, a woodlot or even a few trees suitable for nesting.

Most species of hawks are holding their own today, or even increasing and adapting to human-dominated habitats. The exception are a few species that breed in northern woodlands, such as Sharp-shinned and Broad-winged hawks, which seem to have suffered declines, probably as a result of large-scale deforestation on their home ranges and a decline in prey base. Today, if direct persecution and chemical contamination remain low, habitat loss is the greatest threat to hawk populations anywhere.

The change in attitude toward predators that has taken place during the past few decades is an extreme example of the fickleness of human values toward natural things. In one lifetime, our relationship with birds of prey has progressed from hatred and contempt to admiration and love. Less than half a century ago, hawk shooting was applauded all across North America and hundreds of thousands were killed year after year. Raptors now enjoy extensive legal protection. Millions of dollars have been spent on the recovery of some species, and crowds of enthusiasts gather at migration hotspots nationwide just for the joy of seeing these soaring birds of prey.

Watching hawks leads to surprise and discovery, gives us a glimpse into nature's magic and a delightful escape from our daily lives. These are some of the reasons hawk watching is gaining in popularity. Many exciting discoveries remain to be made—you need only a perceptive eye, an open mind, patience and a little luck.

Red-tails have light-colored eyes that become darker brown with maturity.

REFERENCES

Angell, T. "A Study of the Ferruginous Hawk: Adult and Brood Behavior." *The Living Bird* 8 (1969): 225-241.

Bednarz, J. C. "Social Hunting in Harris' Hawks." In *Birds of Prey*. I. Newton, ed. New York: Facts on File, Inc., 1990.

Bent, A. C. *Life Histories of North American Birds of Prey*, Part I. New York: Dover Publications, 1938.

Brown, L., and D. Amadon. *Eagles, Hawks and Falcons of the World*. Feltham, Middlesex, Great Britain: Hamlyn Publishing Group Limited, 1968.

Cain, S. L., R. N. Smith, and J. R. Dunk. "Blackfly Induced Mortality of Red-tailed Hawk Nestlings in Northwest Wyoming." *Journal of Raptor Research* 27, no. 1 (1993): 66.

Clark, W. S., and B. K. Wheeler. *A Field Guide to Hawks: North America*. Peterson Field Guides Series. Boston: Houghton Mifflin Company, 1987.

Cochran, W. W. "Ocean Migration of Peregrine Falcons: Is the Adult Male Pelagic?" In *Proceedings of Hawk Migration Conference IV*. Hawk Migration Association of North America (1985): 223-237.

Dekker, D. "Migrations of Diurnal Birds of Prey in the Rocky Mountain Foothills, West of Cochrane, Alberta." *Blue Jay* 28 (1970): 20-24.

Dekker, D. *Wild Hunters*. Edmonton: CWD Publications, 1985.

Errington, P. L. *Of Predation and Life*. Ames: Iowa State University Press, 1967.

Grossman, M. L., and J. Hamlet. *Birds of Prey of the World*. New York: Clarkson & Potter Inc., 1964.

Hamerstrom, F. *Harrier: Hawk of the Marshes*. Washington D.C.: Smithsonian Institution Press, 1986.

Heintzelman, D. S. *The Migrations of Hawks*. Indianapolis: Indiana University Press, 1986.

Luttich, S., D. H. Rusch, E. C. Meslow, and L. B. Keith. "Ecology of Red-tailed Hawk Predation in Alberta." *Ecology* 51, no. 2 (1970): 190-203.

Matray, P. F. "Broad-winged Hawk Nesting and Ecology." *Auk* 91 (1974): 307-324.

Newton, I. *Population Ecology of Raptors*. Vermillion, SD: Buteo Books, 1979.

Schnell, G. D. "Communal Roosts of Wintering Rough-legged Hawks." *Auk* 86 (1969): 682-690.

Palmer, R. S. (Ed.) *Handbook of North American Birds, Diurnal Raptors*. Volumes 4 and 5. New Haven and London: Yale University Press, 1988.

Portnoy, J. W., and W. E. Dodge. "Red-shouldered Hawk Nesting Ecology and Behavior." *Wilson Bulletin* 91, no. 1 (1979): 104-117.

Rusch, D. H., and P. D. Doerr. "Broad-winged Hawk Nesting and Food Habits." *Auk* 89 (1972): 139-145.

Schmutz, J. K., K. A. Rose, and R. G. Johnson. 1989. "Hazards to Raptors from Strychnine Poisoned Ground Squirrels." *Journal of Raptor Research* 23, no. 4 (1989): 147-151.

Sprunt, A. *North American Birds of Prey*. New York: Harper & Brothers, 1955.

Wakeley, J. S. "Factors Affecting the Use of Hunting Sites by Ferruginous Hawks." *Condor* 80 (1978): 316-326.

NAMES AND WINGSPAN OF HAWKS FEATURED IN THIS BOOK

Common Name	Latin Name	Wingspan Inches / Centimeters	
Northern Harrier	*Circus cyaneus*	38-48	97-122
Sharp-shinned Hawk	*Accipiter striatus*	20-26	53-65
Cooper's Hawk	*Accipiter cooperii*	28-34	70-87
Northern Goshawk	*Accipiter gentilis*	38-45	98-115
Red-shouldered Hawk	*Asturina lineatus*	37-42	94-107
Red-tailed Hawk	*Buteo jamaicensis*	43-56	110-141
Swainson's Hawk	*Buteo swainsoni*	47-54	120-137
Rough-legged Hawk	*Buteo lagopus*	48-56	122-143
Ferruginous Hawk	*Buteo regalis*	53-60	134-152
Broad-winged Hawk	*Buteo platypterus*	32-36	82-92
Short-tailed Hawk	*Buteo brachyurus*	32-41	83-103
Common Black Hawk	*Buteogallus anthracinus*	40-50	102-128
Zone-tailed Hawk	*Buteo albonotatus*	48-55	121-140
White-tailed Hawk	*Buteo albicaudatus*	49-53	126-135
Gray Hawk	*Buteo nitidus*	2-38	82-98
Roadside Hawk	*Asturina magnirostris*	28-31	72-79
Harris' Hawk	*Parabuteo unicinctus*	40-47	103-119

Latin names, *Handbook Of North American Birds, Diurnal Raptors* (Ed. R. S. Palmer).
Measurements, *A Field Guide To Hawks:North America* (W. S. Clark and B. Wheeler).